Young Learners English

Starters

Practice Tests Plus Teacher's Guide

Rosemary Aravanis

Teaching not just testing

Pearson Education Limited
Edinburgh Gate
Harlow
Essex CM20 2JE
England
and Associated Companies throughout the world.

www.pearsonelt.com

First published 2012
Sixth impression 2018

ISBN: 978-1-4082-9664-6

Set in Sassoon Sans.
Printed in Great Britain by Ashford Colour Press Ltd.

Acknowledgements
The publishers and author would like to thank the following people and institutions for their feedback and comments during the development of the material:

Drew Hyde and Nasser Al Dogom and the Frances King School of English.

Author Acknowledgements
Many thanks to Tessie and Karen for their useful advice and all their hard work. It is much appreciated.

Illustrated by Quadrum Solutions.

Cover Image reproduced here by permission of Cambridge ESOL. This image is drawn from the CYLE Tests Sample Papers, published by Cambridge ESOL, 2006.

Contents

Introduction

The *Young Learners English Practice Tests Plus* series is aimed at students aged 7-12 years who are preparing for the Cambridge Young Learners English Tests. It consists of three levels: *Starters, Movers* and *Flyers*.

The CYLE Tests are suitable for learners of all nationalities whose first language is not English, whatever their cultural background. They cover all four language skills – reading, writing, listening and speaking and include a range of tasks which assess candidates' ability to use and communicate effectively in English. All candidates who complete their test receive an Award, which focuses not on what they *can't* do, but on what they *can* do. The award certificate has a shield score boundary which outlines individual attainment. The Cambridge Young Learners Tests are aligned with the Common European Framework of References for Language, at levels A1 and A2. They also provide an appropriate first step towards the main Cambridge ESOL exams (KET and PET).

■ Components

The components of *Young Learners English Practice Tests Plus* are:

- The **Student's Book** which contains five practice tests. Each test is divided into three sections: Listening, Reading & Writing and Speaking. Teachers may wish to use some of the tests as classroom practise activities before doing the others under exam conditions.
- The **Teacher's Book** which contains an overview and teaching tips for each part of the test; reduced pages of the Student's Book with embedded answers in place; Teaching guidelines for each test; a Speaking frame for each test giving procedures and language to use in each speaking test; 14 photocopiable worksheets with Teacher's Notes; CYLE grammar, structures and vocabulary lists. Test 1 of each level has suggested warm-up activities and worksheets. Teachers can choose when to use these: with Test 1 only or throughout all five tests.
- The **Multi-ROM** which includes the audio for the Listening tests, the audioscripts, a video of Speaking test 1 and video transcripts. The video of the Speaking test on the multi-ROM, together with the Speaking frame in the Teacher's Book, is designed to give teachers a detailed example of how to go about providing students with realistic practice for the Speaking test.

■ Starters Listening Test

Overview

Parts (20 minutes)	What is the skills focus?	What does the child do?
1 (5 questions)	Listening for words and prepositions	Draws lines to position objects correctly on a picture
2 (5 questions)	Listening for numbers and spelling	Writes numbers and names
3 (5 questions)	Listening for specific information	Ticks the correct box under the picture
4 (5 questions)	Listening for words, colours and prepositions	Locates objects in a picture and colours correctly

Guidance

Part 1

- Students should look at the picture and objects before the questions start. They should be encouraged to predict where each object may be placed in the picture.
- Students need to pay attention to the prepositions they hear as these will help them know where to place each object in the picture.
- Encourage them to draw straight lines between the objects and the items in the picture. This will help them to check their answers during the second listening.

Part 2

- Students only need to write a name or a number for each answer.
- Students need to know the range of children's names they are likely to encounter in the test (Boys: *Dan, Alex, Ben, Bill, Nick, Pat, Sam, Tom* and *Tony*. Girls: *Grace, Ann, Anna, Jill, Kim, Lucy, May* and *Sue*).
- All the names come from the Starters vocabulary list (see pages 108–112) and they will be spelt out.
- Students need plenty of practice with the names of letters of the alphabet (they will need to listen and copy them down).
- Students should be encouraged to write numbers as digits as any spelling mistakes will be penalised. Students will only hear numbers 1–20.

They should be given plenty of practice hearing and recognising numbers.

Part 3

- This part covers a wide range of grammar and vocabulary (appropriate to this level). Make sure the vocabulary and structures in the *Starters* syllabus (see pages 107–112) have been well covered on the course.
- Students should listen to the whole dialogue before choosing an answer as the answer may be in several parts of the dialogue.

Part 4

- Students need to have their coloured pencils ready for this.
- Students need to know the range of colours used (*black, blue, brown, green, grey, orange, pink, purple, red, yellow*).
- Students have to listen carefully to indentify which object in the picture is being described.

Teaching Tips

General

- Make sure students know what's expected of them in each part. Read the instructions and listen to the example. Pause to check students understand.
- Always allow students to listen to the recording twice (each recording appears twice in the Audio). If necessary with the first two or three tests, play the recording a third time.
- When checking answers, make use of the audioscript. Give students a copy of it and then play the recording again. Students listen and read to check their answers.

Part 1

- Make sure students can recognise the nouns in the Starters vocabulary list.
- Give students plenty of practice understanding and using prepositional phrases. Make sure they are familiar with the differences between prepositions (e.g. *in* versus *on*).
- Before they listen, ask students to name all the objects surrounding the picture and the objects in the picture.

Part 2

- Before they listen, read the questions together. Make sure they know what type of answer they should write (i.e. a name or a number).
- After they listen, check student's handwriting. Is it legible? If not, give students more handwriting practice.

Part 3

- Give students time to look at the pictures before they listen. If there are people in the pictures, they could say who they may be, where they are and what they are doing. Check students know the names of the items in the pictures.
- Take this opportunity to revise or pre-teach any words they may need to know, e.g. *mango, pineapple,* etc.
- After they listen, ask students to describe one or two pictures.

Part 4

- Before they listen, check students have the correct coloured pencils with them. Check the colours by saying them and asking students to lift the corresponding pencil.
- Check also that they know the name of the items in the picture.
- Ask them to predict what colour they think each item might be.
- After they listen, check that they have chosen the correct colours and items to colour.

■ Starters Reading & Writing Test

Overview

Parts (20 minutes)	What is the skills focus?	What does the child do?
1 (5 questions)	Reading sentences and recognising words	Ticks or crosses to show a sentence is true or false
2 (5 questions)	Reading sentences about a picture Writing one-word answers	Writes yes / no
3 (5 questions)	Spelling of words	Writes words
4 (5 questions)	Reading a text and writing missing words	Chooses and copies missing words correctly
5 (5 questions)	Reading questions about a picture story and answering by writing one word answers	Writes one word answers to questions

Introduction

Guidance

Part 1

- Encourage students to read the sentences and look at the pictures carefully.
- Make sure their ticks look like ticks and their crosses like crosses. Give students practice marking sentences with ticks and crosses.

Part 2

- Give students practice matching *yes* or *no* sentences with pictures.
- Make sure students are familiar with common action verbs, e.g. *run, ride, walk, play, throw, sing*, etc.
- Make sure they understand the meaning of different prepositions, e.g. *in* versus *on*.

Part 3

- Give students practice writing the words in the Starters vocabulary list. Deciphering anagrams can be useful.
- Highlight common letter patterns in words, e.g. *tt, ck, ou, er, ight*.

Part 4

- Tell students to read the whole text first to get a general idea of what it is about.
- Students should read the whole sentence before choosing the right word for the gap. They should then read the completed sentence to see if it makes sense.
- Remind students that the word they choose needs to fit grammatically.

Part 5

- Encourage students to look at the pictures carefully.
- Check they know the names of the objects in the pictures.
- Students should not use more than one word in each gap.

Teaching Tips

General

- Make sure students know what's expected of them in each part: read the instructions and the example and check students understand.
- Marks are often lost because letters and/or words are not written clearly. Students should check that their handwriting is clear and they should be given plenty of handwriting practice. Encourage them to print rather than use joined-up writing, which can be unclear.

- Tell students to write only as much as is needed in each gap. Marks can be lost when students attempt to write more than is necessary, as it often leads to more mistakes being made.
- Teach your young students to manage their time well. Set time limits in class so that they can experience the limited time of the exam. This will help students concentrate and be less distracted by other things.
- Make sure students are familiar with the structures and vocabulary in the *Starters* syllabus (see pages 107–112).

Part 1

- Go through the examples together. Get students to correct the sentences so that they are true.

Part 2

- Before they read the questions, ask students some questions about the picture, e.g. *How many birds can you see? What colour are they?*
- Go through the examples together. Ask students to find evidence in the picture to justify the answers.
- Encourage students to read the sentences carefully and to look very closely at the picture before deciding on an answer. Remind them that the sentence must be completely true for the answer to be *yes*.

Part 3

- Read the instructions carefully and go through the example with the class.
- Tell students that each dash represents a letter in the word.
- After students write their answers, check their handwriting.

Part 4

- Ask students to read the text quickly for the gist. Tell them to ignore the gaps.
- Without looking at the options and pictures, ask students to guess which word could go in each gap. This will help them choose the right word when they do see the options.
- When they have finished, students should read the completed text to see if it makes sense.

Part 5

- Before reading the sentences, ask students to say what's happening in the pictures. They can do this in their own language.
- Go through the examples together as a class.
- Check answers after each section. Ask students to point to the part of the picture that contains the answer.

■ Starters Speaking Test
Overview

Parts (20 minutes)	What is the skills focus?	What does the child do?
1	Understanding and following spoken instructions	Points to the correct part of the picture
2	Understanding and following spoken instructions	Places object cards on the scene picture
3	Understanding and answering spoken questions	Answers questions about scene picture with short answers
4	Understanding and answering spoken questions	Answers questions about three object cards with short answers
5	Understanding and responding to personal questions	Answers personal questions with short answers

Guidance

Part 1
- Students should be given practice identifying people, animals and objects in different pictures. They only need to point in response to questions such as *Where's the table? Where's the elephant?*

Part 2
- Students should be given practice placing smaller pictures (object cards) in different positions on a larger picture (the scene picture). They need to learn how to follow instructions such as *Put the clock on the table.*
- Students need to be familiar with prepositions of place as well as the nouns in the pictures.

Part 3
- Students are only expected to give short answers to the questions, e.g. *How many birds are there? Three / Three birds / There are three birds* are all acceptable answers.
- If students don't understand a question, encourage them to say so.

Part 4
- Students will need to answer questions about objects in pictures. Only simple answers of one or two words are expected.
- Students will need to answer questions about themselves, too, e.g. *What is this?* (a bike) *Have you got a bike? What colour is your bike?*

Part 5
- Students need to be familiar with personal questions on topics such as names, age, family, friends, school, hobbies.
- Again, if they don't understand a question encourage them to ask you to repeat.

Teaching Tips
General
- Make sure students know what's expected of them in each part. They should know that they are required to follow instructions, point or to talk in a very simple way about different pictures and to answer simple questions about themselves.
- Use English in class as much as possible. Students should be familiar with everyday classroom instructions. Teach them how to say *Sorry* or *I don't understand* when appropriate.
- Make sure students are able to use *Hello, Goodbye* and *Thank you.*
- Give students practice following instructions like *Look at..., Give..., Put..., Find...,*
- Work as a class and give students plenty of practice doing each type of task.
- Make sure students are familiar with the structures and vocabulary in the *Starters* syllabus.

Part 1
- Make sure students know the names of the items in the scene picture and the object cards. Ask them some questions, e.g. *Where the tree?* etc.

Part 2
- Make sure students know that they are required to pick up the object card as directed and listen for the instruction of where to put the object card on the scene picture.
- Practice prepositions of place by giving students more instructions where to put each object card, e.g. *Put the clock on the table. Now put the clock under the chair.* etc.

Part 3
- Make sure students are given plenty of practice answering questions about a picture, e.g. *How many birds are there? What is the cat doing?*

Parts 4 and 5
- Make sure students are given plenty of practice answering questions about an object and about themselves, e.g. *What is this?* (It's a bike) *What colour is it?* (It's green) *Have you got a bike?* (yes).
- Give them plenty of practice answering questions about themselves, their families and friends, their homes, their school, their free-time activities and their likes and dislikes, e.g. *How old are you? What's your mum's name? Can you ride a bike?* etc.

Test 1

Listening Part 1

In this part, students listen and correctly position items on a picture by drawing lines.

■ Warm-up

Activity 1

Aim: To practise prepositions of place.

Materials: TB p93 Worksheet 1

Procedure

1 Give out the worksheets.
2 Point to picture 1. Ask *What's this?* (a mouse / a bookcase). Repeat with the other pictures.
3 Point to the prepositions and say each one. Get the students to repeat.
4 The students work individually to look at the pictures and match them to the correct prepositions. Ask them to compare their answers in pairs.
5 Check answers with the class.

Answer Key	
1 in front of	**5** between
2 on	**6** in
3 behind	**7** next to
4 under	

Activity 2

Aim: To practise following instructions containing prepositions of place.

Materials: Various classroom objects (e.g. ruler, rubber, pencil, pen, coloured pencils, course book, notebook, bag, pencil case, sharpener, etc.)

Procedure

1 Ask students to lay out various classroom objects on their desks (they should have cleared their desks before this).
2 Give students instructions as to where to move the objects. Use a variety of prepositions of place, e.g.

Test 1   Listenir

Part 1
– 5 questions –

Listen and draw lines. There is one example.

Test 1, Listening Part 1   5

Put the ruler between the pencil and the notebook.

Now put the rubber under the table.

Put the course book on the chair.

Put the blue pencil next to the red pencil.

3 Put the students into pairs. They should take it in turns to give each other instructions and move the objects accordingly.

Extension

Give out copies of Worksheet 12 and ask questions, e.g. *Where's the lamp?* (on the TV) *Where's the mirror?* (next to the window), etc.

Alternatively, a confident class could work in pairs to ask and answer questions.

■ Do the test

Materials: SB page 5, Audio T1P1

1 Ask students to turn to SB page 5.
2 Point to each of the objects around the picture in turn and ask *What's this?* Get different students to answer, e.g. *It's a hat.*
3 Ask students to name all the items and colours in the picture, e.g. *They're flowers. The sofa is blue.*

4 Play the first part of audio T1P1. Go through the example.

5 Play the rest of the recording and students draw lines to position the objects on the picture.

6 Let students listen to the recording again. Check answers.

Audioscript

R	= rubric
Fch	= Female child
F	= Female adult
Mch	= Male child
M	= Male adult

R **Look at part 1. Now look at the picture. Listen and look. There is one example.**

M Put the juice on the table.

F Sorry? Put the juice where?

M On the table.

F Right!

R **Can you see the line? This is an example. Now you listen and draw lines.**
One

M Put the hat on the boy's head.

F Pardon?

M The hat. Put it on the boy's head.

F Ok.

R **Two**

M Can you see the mango?

F Yes.

M Put the mango under the TV.

F OK, it's under the TV.

R **Three**

M Now put the phone between the flowers and the book.

F Between the flowers and the book? What do I put there?

M The phone.

F OK.

R **Four**

M Put the shoe on the chair.

F Which chair?

M The chair under the window.

F OK. It's on the chair.

R **Five**

M And now put the hippo on the sofa next to the door.

F Pardon? Put it where?

M Put the hippo on the sofa.

F Yes, it's there now.

R **Now listen to Part One again.**

Answer Key ➤ SB page 5

Test 1

Listening Part 2

In this part, students listen and write names or numbers.

■ Warm-up

Activity 1

Aim: To familiarise students with the English names that may appear in the Starters Test.

Materials: TB p94 Worksheet 2

Procedure

1 Give out the worksheets. Read out the names in the first column so that students hear them as well as read them. The students put a tick in the correct column according to whether it is a girl's name, a boy's name or both.

Answer Key

	Girl's name	Boy's name	Both girl's & boy's name
Alex			✓
Ann	✓		
Anna	✓		
Ben		✓	
Bill		✓	
Jill	✓		
Kim			✓
Lucy	✓		
May	✓		
Nick		✓	
Pat			✓
Sam			✓
Sue	✓		
Tom		✓	
Tony		✓	
Dan		✓	
Grace	✓		

2 Spell out the names in random order, e.g. T-O-M.

Part 2
– 5 questions –

Read the question. Listen and write a name or a number. There are two examples.

Examples

What is the girl's name? ___Lucy___

How old is she? ___6___

6   Test 1, Listening Part 2

Students listen and write the names. Check by asking students to write each name on the board.

3 Drill the names. Then ask students to work in pairs, saying the names to each other in turn.

Activity 2

Aim: To practise listening to names being spelt out.

Material: A list of your student's first names

Procedure

1 Explain that you will spell out a name of someone in the class. The person whose name it is should put their hand up, e.g. P-E-T-E-R.

2 Repeat this in a number of lessons. Choose five or six names each time.

Extension

1 Spell out a simple word or a name. The class writes what they hear. Check their spelling.

2 Divide the students into pairs. Give each student a list of five words to spell for their partner. Their partner should not be able to see the words. Students take it in turns to spell out their words.

uestions

How many dolls has Lucy got? _____13 / thirteen_____

What's the dog's name? _____Blue_____

Which class is Lucy in? _____2 / two_____

What's the name of Lucy's school? _____Town_____ School

How many children are in Lucy's class? _____19 / nineteen_____

Encourage them to say *Sorry?* or *Please repeat* if they need to. When they've finished they should compare what their partner has written with their list.

■ Do the test
Materials: SB pages 6 & 7, Audio T1P2

1 Ask students to turn to SB pages 6 & 7. Explain the task and make sure students understand they should write either a name or a number.

2 Play the first part of the recording. Go through the examples.

3 Read the rest of the questions together. Ask students to guess what type of information is missing (i.e. a name or a number).

4 Play the rest of the recording and students listen and write answers.

5 Let students listen to the recording again. Check answers. Make sure the students' handwriting is legible and that they have spelt the names correctly.

Audioscript
R **Part Two. Look at the picture. Listen and write a**

name or a number. **There are two examples.**
F Hello, is this your sister?
Mch Yes. Her name's Lucy
F Can you spell Lucy?
Mch It's L-U-C-Y.
F Very good! And how old is she?
Mch She's six now.
F Pardon?
Mch She's six.
R **Can you see the answers? Now you listen and write a name or a number.**
   One
F She's got a lot of dolls!
Mch Yes, she's got thirteen.
F Thirteen? That is a lot.
Mch She likes dolls!!
R **Two**
F Is that her dog?
Mch Yes, his name's Blue.
F Can you spell that?
Mch Yes, I can. It's B-L-U-E.
R **Three**
F Which class is she in?
Mch She's in class two.
F Two?
Mch Yes. She's got a good teacher.
R **Four**
F What's the name of her school?
Mch She goes to Town School.
F Is that T-O-W-N?
Mch That's right.
R **Five**
F How many children are in her class?
Mch Nineteen.
F Nineteen children? That's a big class!
Mch Yes, it is.
R **Now listen to Part Two again.**

Answer Key ➤ SB page 7

Listening Part 3

In this part, students listen to the dialogue and tick the correct picture.

■ Warm-up

Activity 1

Aim: To match spoken descriptions to pictures.

Materials: SB pages 8 & 9, TB p95 Worksheet 3

Procedure

1 Give out one worksheet to each pair of students. Ask them to cut out the cards. Each student should have one set of cards A-C.

2 Ask them to turn to SB pages 8 and 9.

3 Say a sentence that describes an aspect of one of the pictures in the first row, e.g. *This boy is playing on the computer.* The students should hold up the letter corresponding to the picture you have described (card A).

4 Do this with each set of pictures. You could revisit a set and choose the same picture with a different description, e.g. *The boy is in his bedroom.* (card A).

Activity 2

Aim: To relate words to pictures.

Materials: SB pages 8 & 9

Procedure

1 Ask students to turn to SB pages 8 and 9.

2 Say *Number 3 B.* Ask a student to say a word relating to this picture, i.e. an item in the picture or the colour of something in it, e.g. *boy, tennis.*

3 Put students in pairs to take turns saying the number and letter of a picture and then saying a word.

Part 3
– 5 questions –

Listen and tick (✓) the box. There is one example.

What's Nick doing?

A ☐   B ✓   C ☐

1   Which boy is Tom?

A ☐   B ☐   C ✓

2   Which is Jill's favourite drink?

A ☐   B ✓   C ☐

8   Test 1, Listening Part 3

■ Do the test

Materials: SB pages 8 & 9, Audio T1P3

1 Ask students to turn to SB pages 8 & 9. Read the questions and check students know what they mean.

2 Ask students to look at the pictures and check they know the names of the items (objects, places and colours) in them. Take this opportunity to pre-teach any words they may need to know, e.g. *dog, pineapple, bike,* etc.

3 Ask students to guess what each dialogue will be about.

4 Play the first part of the recording. Go through the example.

5 Play the rest of the recording and students listen and tick the correct picture.

6 Let students listen to the recording again. Check answers. Ask students to describe one or two of the pictures.

What's Tony doing?

A ☐  B ☐  C ☑

Where's the spider?

 A ☑  B ☐  C ☐

Where's the baby's duck?

 A ☐ 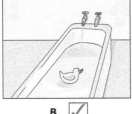 B ☑  C ☐

R	**Three. What's Tony doing?**
F	Is that Tony in the park?
M	Yes. He's with his brother.
F	Is he riding a bike?
M	No, he's reading now.
R	**Four. Where's the spider?**
Fch	Where's the spider now, mum? Is it in the kitchen?
F	No. And it's not in the sitting room.
Fch	Look! It's in the garden.
F	Oh, good. I don't like spiders!
R	**Five. Where's the baby's duck?**
M	Why is the baby crying?
Mch	He can't find his duck in the kitchen.
M	Is it in the bedroom?
Mch	No. Oh look! I can see it now. It's swimming in the bath!
R	**Now listen to Part Three again.**

Answer Key ➤ SB pages 8 & 9

Audioscript

R	**Part Three. Look at the pictures. Now listen and look. There is one example.** **What's Nick doing?**
M	Hello. Is Nick playing with the computer in his bedroom?
Fch	No. He's in the garden.
M	Oh, is he playing football?
Fch	No, he's playing with the dog.
R	**Can you see the tick? Now you listen and tick the box.** **One. Which boy is Tom?**
F	Has Tom got blond hair?
Mch	Yes, and he's wearing a blue T-shirt today.
F	Is he wearing red trousers?
Mch	Yes. Red is his favorite colour.
R	**Two. Which is Jill's favourite drink?**
Mch	Is that orange juice, Jill?
Fch	No it's grape juice.
Mch	Is that your favourite drink?
Fch	No. My favourite is pineapple juice. It's great!

Test 1

Listening Part 4

In this part, the students listen and colour items in a picture.

■ Warm-up

Activity 1

Aim: To practise a colour dictation.

Materials: TB p96 Worksheet 4, coloured pencils

Procedure

1 Revise the colours from the Starters test using coloured pencils, crayons, etc.

2 Give out the worksheets. Give students instructions for colouring the picture, e.g.

Can you see the door?

Colour it blue.

Can you see the tree next to the house?

Colour it green.

Can you see the bag? The one on the chair?

Colour it red.

3 Students compare their finished pictures with their classmates.

4 Students could work in pairs and give each other instructions to colour other items in the picture.

Activity 2

Aim: To practise colouring a picture.

Materials: Sheets of paper (or notebooks), coloured pencils

Procedure

1 Draw a simple picture on the board, e.g. a bedroom with a table, chair, bed, bookcase, toy dog on bed, toy cat under chair, clock on table, book in bookcase. Ask students to copy it in their notebooks.

2 Put them in pairs and they take turns giving each other colouring instructions. This can

Part 4
– 5 questions –

Listen and colour. There is one example.

10   Test 1, Listening Part 4

be very simple, e.g. *Colour the book green* or *The book – green.*

Extension

In later lessons you could use the scene pictures in Worksheets 9 and 12 to practise colour dictations.

■ Do the test

Materials: SB page 10, Audio T1P4, coloured pencils

1 Ask students to turn to SB page 10. Read the instructions together.

2 Check students have all the colours they will need. Check by calling out the colours and

asking students to hold up the corresponding coloured pencil.

3 Check students know the name of the items in the picture.

4 Ask them to predict what colour they think each item will be.

5 Play the first part of the recording. Go through the example.

6 Play the rest of the recording and students listen and colour the picture.

7 Let students listen to the recording again. Check answers.

Audioscript

R   **Part Four. Look at the picture. Listen and look. There is one example.**

F   Look at the banana on the mat.

Mch   Pardon?

F   The banana on the mat. Can you colour it yellow?

Mch   Ok. I'm colouring it yellow.

R   **Can you see the yellow banana on the mat? This is an example. Now you listen and colour.**

     One

F   Can you see the chair?

Mch   Yes. There's a banana on it.

F   Colour that banana blue.

Mch   Right. The banana on the chair is blue now. That's funny!

R   **Two**

F   Look. There's a banana next to the flowers.

Mch   Yes. Can I colour it?

F   Ok. Colour it purple.

Mch   Right. The banana next to the flowers is purple.

R   **Three**

F   Now find the cupboard.

Mch   There's a banana in it.

F   Yes. Colour that banana green.

Mch   Ok. I'm colouring the banana in the cupboard green.

R   **Four**

F   The cat's playing with a banana!

Mch   Yes. It's a toy banana.

F   Oh. Colour that orange, like a carrot.

Mch   Ok. It's orange now.

R   **Five**

F   Look. There's a banana between the apples and the books.

Mch   Yes, I can see it.

F   Colour it red.

Mch   Right. The banana between the apples and the books is red now.

F   Well done. The picture looks good.

R   **Now listen to Part Four again.**

Answer Key ➤ SB page 10

Test 1

Reading & Writing
Part 1

In this part, students look at the picture, read the sentence and put a tick or a cross depending on whether it is true or false.

■ Warm-up

Activity 1

Aim: To give students practice associating words with pictures.

Materials: TB p97 & 98 Worksheets 5 and 6

Procedure

1 Cut up the flashcards on Worksheets 5 and 6.

2 Divide the board into two sections. Put the flashcards from Worksheet 5 on the left hand side of the board in a random order. Write sentences about the pictures (e.g. *This is a lamp, This is baseball,* etc.) in a random order on the right hand side of the board.

3 Ask students, one at a time, to come up and match a picture to a sentence. The rest of the class says *Yes* or *No,* if the student is right or wrong. If they are right, they should tick the sentence on the board (check their tick looks like a tick), if they are wrong, they rub out their matching line.

4 Repeat with another student until all the pictures have been matched.

5 Repeat the activity with the flashcards on Worksheet 6.

Activity 2

Aim: To play pelmanism (a memory game).

Materials: TB p99 & 100 Worksheets 7 & 8

Procedure

1 Put the students into small groups.

2 Give each group a copy of Worksheets 7 & 8 and ask them to cut out the cards.

3 They then turn the picture cards and word cards face down. The students take turns turning two cards at a time. If the two cards match (i.e. the picture of the horse with *horse*), the student keeps the cards.

4 Continue until all the cards are gone. The student with the most cards wins.

■ Do the test

Materials: SB pages 11 & 12

1 Ask students to turn to SB pages 11 & 12. Read the instructions together.

2 Write the example sentences on the board. Underline the key word in each (e.g. *burger, orange*). Ask students to correct the second example sentence, e.g. (*This is a) carrot.*

3 Students underline the key word in the rest of the sentences and decide if the sentences are correct or not.

4 Ask students to compare answers in pairs.

5 Check answers. Students correct the false sentences. (*1 This is a cat. 3 This is a foot.*)

Answer Key ➤ SB pages 11 & 12

Part 1
– 5 questions –

Look and read. Put a tick (✓) or a cross (X) in the box.
There are two examples.

Examples

This is a burger.

This is an orange.

Questions
1

This is a cow.

Test 1

2 This is a doll. ✓

3 This is a sock. ✗

4 This is a fish. ✓

5 This is a watermelon. ✓

12 Test 1, Reading & Writing Part 1

Reading & Writing

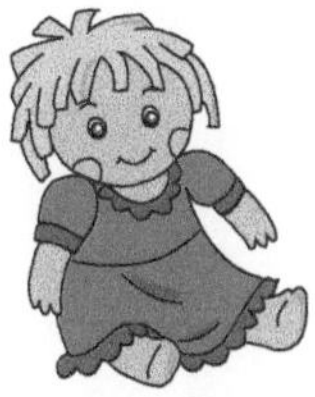

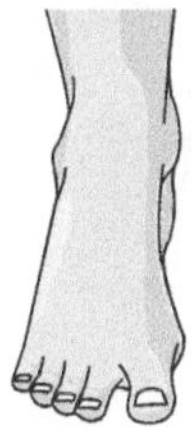

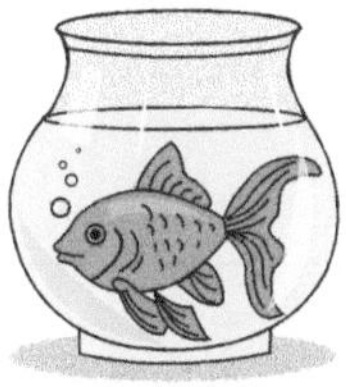

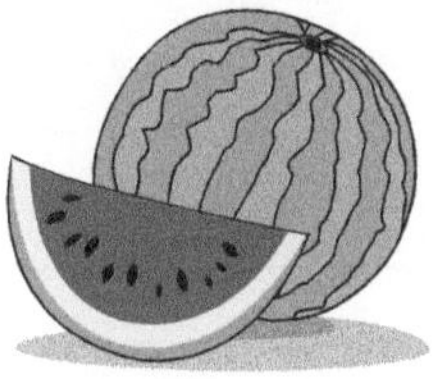

Test 1

Reading & Writing
Part 2

In this part, students look at a picture, read the sentences and then write *yes* or *no*, depending on whether they are true or false.

■ Warm-up

Activity 1

Aim: To practise answering questions with *yes / no* answers.

Materials: None

Procedure

1 Say *Look at our classroom.* Then say *There's a teacher in the classroom.* Encourage the students to say *yes* or *no* depending on whether they think it is true or false.

2 Check the answer and see how many students got it correct.

3 Repeat with other statements appropriate to your classroom, e.g. *There's a big window. There are twelve desks. One boy is reading a book. The clock on the wall is black. There's a girl wearing a red t-shirt. This boy (or use name) has got a blue watch. The brown book is next to the board.*

Activity 2

Aim: To practise reading sentences carefully and writing one word answers.

Materials: TB p101 Worksheet 9

Procedure

1 Give out copies of Worksheet 9 – one per pair would do.

2 Say *Look at the beach.* Ask *What's this?* and point to a few items, e.g. *sun, sea, sand.*

3 Write three true sentences about the picture and three false ones on the board. The sentences should be descriptive, e.g. *There are two*

children in the sea, A woman is sleeping, etc.

4 The students work alone. They read silently and decide if the sentences are true or false and then write *yes* or *no*. They then compare their answers in pairs.

5 Check answers with the class.

Extension

Ask students to correct the false sentences.

■ Do the test

Materials: SB page 13

1 Ask students to turn to SB page 13. Ask them some

questions about the picture, e.g. *How many children can you see? What colour are the flowers?*

2 Discuss the examples together. Ask students to find evidence in the picture to justify the answers.

3 Give students some time to read the descriptions and to check that they match what is happening in the picture.

4 Ask students to compare answers in pairs.

5 Check answers. Students correct the false sentences.

Answer Key ➤ SB page 13

Part 2
– 5 questions –

Look and read. Write yes or no.

Examples

There are four children in the room. _____ *yes*

There is a dog under the table. _____ *no*

Questions

1 There is a mouse in the room. _____ *yes*

2 A boy is playing with a train. _____ *no*

3 There are blue flowers on the bookcase. _____ *no*

4 A baby is holding a ball. _____ *yes*

5 The children are watching television. _____ *no*

Test 1, Reading & Writing Part 2   13

Part 3
– 5 questions –

ook at the pictures. Look at the letters. Write the words.

xample

 b o o k

Questions

 d e s k

 b o a r d

 c h a i r

 p e n c i l

 e r a s e r

14 Test 1, Reading & Writing Part 3

Reading & Writing Part 3

In this part, students reorder letters and write words.

■ Warm-up

Activity 1

Aim: To practise unscrambling anagrams.

Materials: TB p102 Worksheet 10

Procedure

1 Cut out the flashcards on Worksheet 10. Put the six flashcards on the board.

2 Write an anagram of the word next to each picture:

i a f g r f c

g e g

r o r r i m

u e r r l

a n i p o

d n b m t n a o i

3 Give students two minutes to unscramble the anagrams. Check answers by asking students to come up and write the correct words on the board.

Reading & Writing

Answer Key

giraffe	ruler
egg	piano
mirror	badminton

Extension

You could repeat the activity using the flashcards on Worksheets 5 & 6.

Activity 2

Aim: To practise making up their own anagrams.

Materials: A sheet of paper for each student (or their notebooks)

Procedure

1 Ask students to create their own anagrams for six words you have recently learnt in class.

2 They then swap anagrams with another student and try to unscramble each other's. Students can work alone or in pairs to do this.

■ Do the test

Materials: SB page 14

1 Ask students to turn to SB page 14. Read the instructions carefully. Explain that each dash represents a letter and that the pictures should help them.

2 Write the example on the board. Write both the jumbled letters and the word spelt correctly.

3 Give students some time to unscramble the rest of the jumbled words. Encourage them to cross out the letters after they have used them. Remind them to write only one letter in each space.

4 Ask students to compare answers in pairs.

5 Check answers. Check students have spelt the words correctly.

Answer Key ➤ SB page 14

Test 1

Reading & Writing Part 4

In this part, students read a text and complete it with the missing words.

■ Warm-up

Activity 1

Aim: To practise writing missing words.

Materials: TB p102 Worksheet 10

Procedure

1 Put the flashcards on the board along the top. Point to each one and get students to say the word, e.g. *giraffe*.

2 Write a sentence on the board with a gap which one of the flashcard words could fit in, e.g. *A _____ has got long legs. (giraffe)*
I can play the _____ . (piano)

3 Ask individual students to suggest which flashcard it could be, the others agree or not. (Sometimes more than one flashcard might fit.)

4 Rub this out and repeat with another flashcard and sentence.

Extension

Repeat the activity with the flashcards from Worksheets 5 and 6. If you have confident students, they could work in pairs to write the gapped sentences.

Activity 2

Aim: To familiarise students with gap-fill texts.

Materials: TB p103 Worksheet 11

Procedure

1 Give out the top part of the worksheet.

2 Ask students to read the title and to say what the text is about (*a monkey*).

Part 4
– 5 questions –

Read this. Choose a word from the box. Write the correct word next to the numbers 1–5. There is one example.

A monkey

I live in the _____ trees _____ with my family and friends. I play with them a lo

In the morning I eat a **(1)** _____ banana _____ . I love it! It's my favourite food.

I am small and I have a long **(2)** _____ tail _____ . I can run and I can jump

but I can't use a **(3)** _____ computer _____ .

I can't read a **(4)** _____ book _____ and I don't go to **(5)** _____ school _____ .

What am I? I am a monkey.

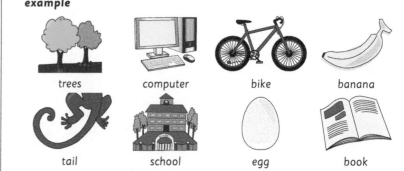

example

trees   computer   bike   banana

tail   school   egg   book

Test 1, Reading & Writing Part 4   15

3 Discuss the example as a class. Ask them why it is a good answer. Ask them if they can think of any other words which would fit.

4 Put the students into pairs. Ask them to read the text carefully and to guess what the missing words might be. Get feedback but don't confirm or refute any answers at this stage.

5 Write one or two of their suggestions on the board next to the numbers 1–5.

Extension

In future lessons, give out the bottom part of Worksheet 11. Students work in pairs to choose the correct words to write in the gaps. Go through the answers with the class.

■ Do the test

Materials: SB page 15

1 Ask students to turn to SB page 15. Ask students to read the instructions to the task and then ask the following questions (in L1 if necessary):
How many words do you write in each gap? (one)

Where can you find the words? (in the box)

Can you write a word that isn't in the box? (no)

How many words are there in the box? (eight)

How many gaps are there in the text? (five, plus one example)

How many extra words are there? (two)

2 Ask them to say what the text is about. The picture and title will help them. (If you have done Activity 2 above, students will know the answer to this.)

3 Discuss the example together. Ask them to cross out the word and picture in the box that was used in the example.

4 Give students some time to read the text carefully and to try to choose the best word from the box for each gap. Tell them to read the whole sentence before deciding on the best word for a gap.

5 Ask students to compare answers in pairs.

6 Check answers.

7 If you did Warm-up Activity 2, check if the answers matched their suggestions on the board.

Answer Key ➤ SB page 15

Test 1

Reading & Writing Part 5

In this part, students look at a picture and then write one-word answers to questions.

■ Warm-up

Activity 1

Aim: To practise giving short answers to questions about a picture.

Materials: TB p104 Worksheet 12

Procedure

1 Give out the worksheets.

2 Write about four–six questions on the board about it, e.g.

   How many children are there?

   What is the girl doing?

   How many flowers are there?

   Where is the lamp?

   What's the man wearing?

   Where is the mirror?

   If an answer requires more than a one-word answer, write the beginning of the answer next to the question (e.g. for the fourth question above write *on the…* and for the sixth write *next to the …*).

3 The students read the questions carefully and write one-word answers.

4 Ask students to pair up with another student. They should agree on the best answer for each question.

5 The students should form groups by pairing up with another pair of students. They should agree on the best answer for each question.

6 Ask groups to appoint a representative to come up to the board and write their group's answers next to the questions. Discuss the answers as a class.

Part 5
– 5 questions –

Look at the pictures and read the questions. Write one-word answers.

Examples

Where are the people?	in the _____ street
How many shops are there?	_____ three

Questions

1 What is the woman holding?	a _____ handbag

16   Test 1, Reading & Writing Part 5

Answer Key

(for example questions above)

2 / two

reading

3 / three

TV / television

glasses / trousers / shirt / shoes

window

Activity 2

Aim: To practise asking and answering questions about a picture.

Materials: TB p101 Worksheet 9, or a picture from your coursebook

Procedure

1 Ask the students to work in small groups. Give out a copy of the worksheet to each group.

2 Ask them to write five questions about their picture, e.g. *Where is the dog? What is the girl in the sea doing? Who is drinking?* etc. Give students five to ten minutes to do this. Monitor and help if needed.

Where are the jeans?   on the _____ *chair*

What is the girl in the blue
dress looking at?   at a _____ *(red) t-shirt*

Where are the people now?   in front of a _____ *house*

What are they holding?   some big _____ *bags*

Test 1, Reading & Writing Part 5   17

3 Ask groups to swap questions with another group. The students should answer the other group's questions. When they have finished, they should swap answers with the other group and correct each other's work.

■ Do the test
Materials: SB pages 16 & 17

1 Ask students to turn to SB pages 16 & 17. Ask them to name the items in the pictures. Pre-teach any they don't know.

2 Read the instructions carefully and discuss the examples together. Ask students to point to the parts of the picture that contain the answers.

3 Give students time to read the questions and write the answers. Remind them to write only one-word answers.

4 Check answers after each section. Ask students to compare answers in pairs first. When checking the answers, make sure students have spelt with words correctly.

Answer Key ➤ SB pages 16 & 17

Test 1

Speaking Part 1

In this part, students point to items on the scene picture.

■ Warm-up

Activity 1

Aim: To practise listening to *Where* questions and pointing to items in the classroom.

Materials: Classroom objects (e.g. *pen, pencil, ruler, rubber, picture, board, pencil case, books,* etc.), other items (e.g. *fruit, toys, pictures,* etc.)

Procedure

1. Place a selection of classroom objects in visible positions around the class, e.g. some can be under the desk, on a cupboard, on a window sill, etc. as long as they are visible to the students. You might also want to bring in some items from home (such as toys or fruit) and place these in different positions around the room.

2. Ask students questions about the location of the objects. The students should respond by pointing. For example:

   Where's the board? (students point)

   Where are the books? (students point)

   Where are the pictures? (students point)

   Where's the bear? (students point)

   Where's the apple? (students point)

3. You could ask confident students to come up and take your role of asking the questions.

Activity 2

Aim: To practise asking *Where* questions and pointing to items on a picture.

Object cards

 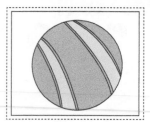

Materials: TB p96 Worksheet 4 (one copy per pair)

Procedure

1. Put the students into pairs and give each pair a copy of Worksheet 4.

2. Demonstrate by saying *Where's the tree?* and then pointing to it on the picture.

3. In their pairs, the students now take turns to ask *Where* questions and point to items on the picture.

■ Do the test

Materials: SB page 21

1. Check students know the names of items in the scene picture.

2. Ask them some questions about the scene picture. The students should point to the items rather than describe where each item is, e.g.

   Where is the cat?

   Where is the car?

   Where are the children?

   etc.

Scene picture

Test 1, Speaking Parts 1–3　21

Put the bag next to the door.
Where is the ruler?
Put the ruler in the cupboard. etc.

4 The rest of the class should check that the student is pointing and responding appropriately. Give all students a chance to point and carry out the instruction.

Activity 2
Aim: To practise placing picture cards in various positions.
Materials: TB p99 Worksheet 7
Procedure

1 Put students in pairs and give each pair a set of picture cards from Worksheet 7.

2 The students lay the picture cards face up in front of them.

3 They then take it in turns to ask each other questions and give each other instructions, e.g. *Where's the hat? Point to the eye. Put the cake under the clock. Put the shell next to the baby.*

Extension
You could give out copies of Worksheet 12 and ask pairs to place cards on the picture, e.g. *Put the hat on the table.*

■ Do the test
Materials: SB page 19

1 Ask students to lay out the object cards on their desk.

2 Give students instructions where to put some of the object cards, e.g.
Which is the guitar?
Put the guitar on the sun.
Which is the apple?
Put the apple between the dog and the children.
Which is the ball?
Put the ball under the tree.
Which is the frog?
Put the frog next to the mouse.
etc.

Speaking Part 2

In this part, students put the object cards in various locations on the scene picture.

■ Warm-up

Activity 1
Aim: To practise responding physically to instructions.
Materials: Classroom and household objects
Procedure

1 Put some objects on a table that all students can see. The objects can be classroom objects but they can also be smaller objects

you bring in from home (e.g. *a box, a cup, an apple, a sock*, etc.).

2 Get a student to come out to the front. Ask a *Where* question, e.g. *Where is the pencil?* and encourage the student to point to the pencil. Then give an instruction (a simple sentence with an object and a preposition of place), e.g. *Put the pencil under your chair.* The student carries out the action.

3 Repeat with other students and instructions:
Where is the box?
Put the box on your table.
Where is the bag?

Test 1, Speaking Part 2　25

Speaking Part 3

In this part, students answer questions about people or things in the scene picture.

■ Warm-up

Activity 1

Aim: To practise answering questions with short one-word answers.

Materials: Classroom objects (e.g. *pen, pencil, ruler, rubber, picture, board, pencil case, books,* etc.), other items (e.g. *fruit, toys, pictures,* etc.)

Procedure

1 Point to an item in the classroom and ask *What's this?* Get a student to answer, e.g. *a pencil.* Then ask *What colour is it?* Get a different student to answer, e.g. *red.*

2 Repeat with other items and other questions, such as *What are these? How many books are there? How many pictures are there? What colour is the bear?*

Extension

Ask a student to come up to the front of the class. He / She should ask the class some questions. Alternatively, students work in groups. They take it in turns to ask each other questions and to answer them.

Activity 2

Aim: To practise answering questions about a picture with one-word answers.

Materials: TB p101 Worksheet 9

Procedure

1 Give out the worksheets.

2 Ask *What's the old man doing?* or *What's this boy doing?* (and then point to the boy in the sea).

3 Encourage students to reply with one word answers, e.g. *walking / swimming.*

4 Put the students in pairs and they take turns asking the question and saying the one-word answer (which should always end in *–ing*).

■ Do the test

Materials: SB page 21

1 Ask students some questions about the scene picture. These questions should be ones that the students will need to answer verbally, e.g.

What's this? (a flower) *What colour is it?* (red and yellow)

How many flowers are there? (five)

Where is the baby? (the students point to the baby)

What is the baby doing? (he's sleeping)

Speaking Part 4

In this part, students answer questions about the object cards.

■ Warm-up

Activity 1

Aim: To practise answering questions about objects in pictures.

Materials: TB p105 Worksheet 13

Procedure

1 Give students a copy of the worksheet. Ask them to complete the gaps with the name of the object in each picture.

2 Students should then write answers to the questions.

3 Ask them to work in pairs. They take it in turns to ask each other the questions and answer them. If possible, they should try to do this without looking at the questions and answers.

4 Ask some of the questions to individual students.

Answer Key	
a socks	**b** dog
c bread	**d** telephone

Activity 2

Aim: To practise asking and answering questions about objects in pictures.

Materials: The object cards from a speaking test or the picture cards on Worksheets 5, 6 or 10

Procedure

1 Ask students to work in pairs. Give each pair a set of cards.

2 One student is the examiner and the other the candidate. The examiner should ask the candidate some questions about some of the cards, e.g.

What's this? (e.g. (it's an) apple)

What colour is it? (e.g. (it's) green)

Do you like apples? (e.g. yes)

What's your favourite food? (e.g. chips and pizza)

3 Allow them a few minutes to do this and then ask them to swap roles. Monitor and listen. At the end, you could ask some of the pairs to perform in front of the class. Ask the class to give each pair feedback at the end.

■ Do the test

Materials: SB page 19

1 Ask students about the other object cards (the ones not referred to in Part 2), e.g.

What's this? (a jacket)

What colour is it? (grey)

Do you like ice cream? (yes / no)

What do you drink for breakfast? (water, milk, etc.)

Speaking Part 5

In this part, students answer personal questions.

■ Warm-up

Activity 1

Aim: To practise answering personal questions.

Materials: TB p106 Worksheet 14

Procedure

1 Cut out the questions on Worksheet 14.

2 Put students into pairs. Give each pair a set of question cards. They should place them face down on their desk.

3 Students take it in turns to pick up a question card and to ask their partner the question on it, e.g. *Can you play table tennis?* Their partner must answer. Encourage them to answer with more than one word if they can, e.g. *Yes, I can.*

4 Remind students to ask for repetition if they need to hear a question again, e.g. *Sorry? Please can you repeat? I don't understand.* etc.

Activity 2

Aim: To do a role play with personal questions.

Materials: none

Procedure

1 Ask a confident student to come up to the front and demonstrate the following simple role play:

   T: Hello.

   S: Hello.

   T: What's your name?

   S: (Anna).

   T: How old are you?

   S: I'm (eight).

   T: What's your favourite animal?

   S: A dog.

   T: Thank you, Anna. Goodbye.

   S: Goodbye.

2 Put the students in pairs and ask them to do a similar role play, taking it in turns to be the teachers and the student. Encourage them to ask different questions and to add extra questions if they can.

If necessary, write example questions on the board or tell them to refer to the question cards from Worksheet 14.

3 Go round monitoring and helping where necessary.

4 Ask a few pairs to come to the front and demonstrate their role play.

■ Do the test

Materials: None

1 Ask each student some questions about themselves. They can give one-word answers but encourage them to give a longer answer if they can, e.g.

   How old are you? (I'm 10 years old.)

   What's your friend's name? (John)

   How old is he / she? (10)

   Where do you go with your friend? (school)

   Can you play football? (yes / no)

Test 1

Speaking frame (Timing = 5 minutes)

What to do (use child's name throughout the test)	What to say	Answer from candidate (one word sufficient)	Back up question if necessary
Usher brings candidate into examination room	Introduces the child to the examiner: *This is …* Examiner to candidate: *Hello my name's ….*	*Hello*	
1 Examiner opens candidate booklet and shows scene to the candidate.	*Look at this. This is a street. There are some people and the sun is shining.* *This is a cat. (pointing)* *Where is the car?* *Where are the children?*	*Points to items*	*Is this the car? (point)* *Are these the children?*
2 Point to the object cards laid out on the table.	*Look at these, (name).* *Which is the guitar?* *I'm putting the guitar on the cat.* *Now you put the guitar on the sun.* *Which is the watermelon /apple?* *Now put the watermelon / apple between the dog and the children.* *Which is the ball / frog? Put the ball under the tree.*	*Candidate points.* *Examiner puts guitar on the cat.* *Candidate puts card on sun.* *Candidate points.* *Candidate puts card between the dog and the children.* *Candidate points and places the card under the tree.*	*Where is the sun? On the sun.* *Is this the watermelon /apple? (points)* *Between the dog and the children.* *Is this the ball / frog? (points) Under the tree.*
3 Remove the cards and point to the scene. Point to a flower. Point to baby. Remove scene picture.	*What's this?* *What colour is it?* *How many flowers are there?* *What's the baby doing?*	*Flower* *Red and yellow* *Five* *Sleeping*	*Is it a flower?* *Is it blue or yellow?* *Is there one or two?* *Is the baby sleeping?*
4 Take 3 object cards not used previously. Show jacket card. Show ice cream card. Show goat card. Put away all cards.	*What's this?* *What colour is it?* *Have you got a jacket?* *What's this?* *Do you like ice cream?* *What do you drink for breakfast?* *What's this?* *Have you got a cat?* *What's your favourite animal?*	*Jacket* *Grey* *Yes / no* *Ice cream* *Yes / no* *Water* *Goat* *Yes / no* *Horse*	*Is it a jacket?* *Is it grey?* *Is it an ice cream?* *Do you drink milk?* *Is it a goat?* *Do you like cats?*
5 Ask a few personal questions.	*Now, (name). What's your friend's name?* *How old is he / she?* *Where do you go with your friend?*	*Mary / John* *10* *School*	*Is your friend's name, Mary?* *Is he / she 8?* *Do you go to the park?*
	Thank you, (name). *Bye Bye.*		

Part 1
– 5 questions –

Listen and draw lines. There is one example.

Test 2, Listening Part 1   23

Audioscript

R	**Look at part 1. Now look at the picture. Listen and look. There is one example.**
F	Put the ball next to the frog.
M	Sorry? Put the ball where?
F	Next to the frog.
M	Right.
R	**Can you see the line? This is an example. Now you listen and draw lines.**
	One
F	Put the kite between the blue birds.
M	Pardon? Where do I put the kite?
F	Between the blue birds.
M	Right.
R	**Two**
F	Now put the mouse in front of the bike.
M	Sorry, put the mouse where?
F	Put it in front of the bike.
M	Right, I can do that.
R	**Three**
F	And now put the helicopter on the horse's head.
M	The helicopter?
F	Yes, put it on the horse's head.
M	Right, I'm doing that now.
R	**Four**
F	Now put the doll in the bag.
M	Where?
F	Put the doll in the bag.
M	Ok, good.
R	**Five**
F	And now put the tomato under the tree.
M	Sorry, put the tomato where?
F	Put it under the tree.
M	Yes, ok.
R	**Now listen to Part One again.**

Answer Key ➤ SB page 23

Test 2

Listening Part 1

In this part, students listen and correctly position items on a picture by drawing lines.

■ Warm-up
For suggested warm-up activities see Test 1 page 8.

■ Do the test
Materials: SB page 23, Audio T2P1

1 Ask students to turn to SB page 23.
2 Point to each of the objects around the picture in turn and ask *What's this?* Get different students to answer, e.g. *It's a ball.*
3 Ask students to name all the items and colours in the picture, e.g. *They're birds. They're blue.*
4 Play the first part of the recording. Go through the example.
5 Play the rest of the recording and students draw lines to position the objects on the picture.
6 Let students listen to the recording again. Check answers.

Test 2

Listening Part 2

In this part, students listen and write names or numbers.

■ Warm-up

For suggested warm-up activities see Test 1 page 10.

■ Do the test

Materials: SB pages 24 & 25, Audio T2P2

1 Ask students to turn to SB pages 24 & 25. Explain the task and make sure students understand they should write either a name or a number.

2 Play the first part of the recording. Go through the examples.

3 Read the rest of the questions together. Ask students to guess what type of information is missing (i.e. a name or a number).

4 Play the rest of the recording and students listen and write answers.

5 Let students listen to the recording again. Check answers. Make sure the students' handwriting is legible and that they have spelt the names correctly.

Audioscript

R	**Look at the picture. Listen and write a name or a number. There are two examples.**
M	Hello. What's your name?
Fch	It's Anna.
M	Can you spell that?
Fch	Yes. It's A-N-N-A.
M	How old are you, Anna?
Fch	I'm eight.
M	Wow! Eight. Do you go to school?
Fch	Yes. I do.

Part 2
– 5 questions –

Read the question. Listen and write a name or a number.
There are two examples.

Examples

What's the girl's name? _____ *Anna*

How old is she? _____ *8*

R	**Can you see the answers? Now you listen and write a name or a number.**
	One
Fch	Look at this photo. It's my mum.
M	Oh! What's her name?
Fch	It's Sue.
M	Is that S-U-E?
Fch	Sue. Yes. That's right.
R	**Two**
M	Is this your brother?
Fch	Yes. He's a baby. He's two!
M	Pardon. How old is he?

Fch	He's two and he can talk now.
R	**Three**
M	What's his name?
Fch	Alex. Like my dad.
M	Can you spell it?
Fch	Yes. A-L-E-X.
M	Good!
R	**Four**
M	Have you got a sister too, Anna?
Fch	Yes, I have.
M	What's her name?
Fch	Her name's Kim.

...uestions

What is Anna's mum's name? _____ Sue _____

How old is Anna's brother? _____ 2 / two _____

What's his name? _____ Alex _____

What's the name of Anna's sister? _____ Kim _____

How old is Anna's sister? _____ 11 / eleven _____

M	What a nice name! Can you spell it?
Fch	K-I-M.
M	Thanks.
R	**Five**
M	How old is your sister?
Fch	She's eleven.
M	Eleven! She isn't a baby.
Fch	No, she's my big sister.
R	**Now listen to Part Two again.**

Answer Key ➤ SB page 25

Test 2

Listening Part 3

In this part, students listen to the dialogue and tick the correct picture.

■ Warm-up

For suggested warm-up activities see Test 1 page 12.

■ Do the test

Materials: SB pages 26 & 27, Audio T2P3

1 Ask students to turn to SB pages 26 & 27. Read the questions and check students know what they mean.

2 Ask students to look at the pictures and check they know the names of the items (objects, places and colours) in them. Take this opportunity to pre-teach any words they may need to know, e.g. *computer, living room, pear,* etc.

3 Ask students to guess what each dialogue will be about.

4 Play the first part of the recording. Go through the example.

5 Play the rest of the recording and students listen and tick the correct picture.

6 Let students listen to the recording again. Check answers. Ask students to describe one or two of the pictures.

Audioscript

R **Look at the pictures. Now listen and look. There is one example.**
Which girl is Ann?

M Is that Ann wearing a blue dress?

F No, that's Ann's sister. Ann's near the window.

M In a t-shirt and trousers?

F Yes. That's her. She's talking to the girl with the blue T-shirt.

Part 3
– 5 questions –

Listen and tick (✓) the box. There is one example.

Which girl is Ann?

 A ☐    B ☐    C ✓

1   What's Bill's favourite toy?

 A ✓    B ☐   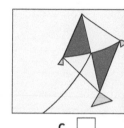 C ☐

2   What's Pat's grandfather doing?

 A ☐    B ✓    C ☐

26   Test 2, Listening Part 3

R **Can you see the tick? Now you listen and tick the box.**
One. What's Bill's favourite toy?

M What toys do you like, Bill?

Mch Robots are OK.

M Do you like kites?

Mch No, I don't. That monkey is my favourite toy. I take it to bed with me!

R **Two. What's Pat's grandfather doing?**

Mch Is your grandfather reading in the house, Pat?

Fch No. He's in the park.

Mch Is he reading in the park?

Fch No. He's walking the dog. They love the park!

R **Three. What can May do?**

Mch May, can you play the guitar?

Fch No, I can't. Sorry.

Mch Can you ride a bike?

Fch No, I can't, but I can play computer games.

R **Four. What does Grace want?**

Fch What fruit have we got mum?

F There's an apple. Do you want that? Or there's a banana.

What can May do?

A ✓   B ☐   C ☐

What does Grace want?

  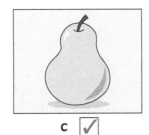

A ☐   B ☐   C ✓

Where's the television?

  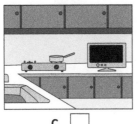

A ✓   B ☐   C ☐

Fch	No thanks. Can I have a pear?
F	Ok. Here you are.
R	**Five. Where's the television?**
Fch	Have you got a television in your bedroom, Tom?
Mch	No, I haven't.
Fch	Is there one in the kitchen?
Mch	No, our television is in the living room.
R	**Now listen to Part Three again.**

Answer Key ➤ SB pages 26 & 27

Test 2

Listening Part 4

In this part, the students listen and colour items in a picture.

■ Warm-up

For suggested warm-up activities see Test 1 page 14.

■ Do the test

Materials: SB page 28, Audio T2P4, coloured pencils

1 Ask students to turn to SB page 28. Read the instructions.
2 Check students have all the colours they will need.
3 Check students know the name of the items in the picture. Ask them to predict what colour they think each item will be.
4 Play the first part of the recording. Go through the example.
5 Play the rest of the recording and students listen and colour the picture.
6 Let students listen to the recording again. Check answers.

Audioscript

R	**Look at the picture. Listen and look. There is one example.**
M	Look at this picture.
Fch	There are some monkeys in the garden!
M	Now. Can you see the monkey with the cat?
Fch	Yes. I can see it. Can I colour its hat purple?
M	Yes, please. The monkey with the cat. Colour its hat purple.
R	**Can you see the monkey with the purple hat? This is an example. Now you listen and colour.**
	One
M	Oh. There's a monkey on a bike. Can you see it?
Fch	Yes, I can.
M	Can you colour that monkey's hat green?
Fch	Ok. The monkey on the bike. Its hat is green now.

Part 4
– 5 questions –

Listen and colour. There is one example.

28   Test 2, Listening Part 4

R	**Two**
Fch	Look at that monkey. She's playing with a doll!
M	Oh, yes. I like her doll.
Fch	Can I colour her hat blue?
M	Yes, blue is a good colour for her hat.
R	**Three**
Fch	What now?
M	Can you see the monkey in the tree?
Fch	Oh yes, I can. It's got long arms!
M	Colour that Monkey's hat red.
Fch	Right. The monkey in the tree has got a red hat now.

R	**Four**
Fch	Look at the monkey with the flowers.
M	Yes the flowers are very nice!
Fch	Can I colour that monkey's hat pink?
M	Yes please. Colour its hat pink.
R	**Five**
Fch	That monkey is eating a banana. Can I colour its hat?
M	Yes. What colour?
Fch	My favourite colour is orange.
M	OK. The monkey with a banana. Colour its hat orange.
Fch	It's a great picture now!
R	**Now listen to Part Four again.**

Answer Key ➤ SB page 28

Part 1
– 5 questions –

Look and read. Put a tick (✓) or a cross (✗) in the box.

Here are two examples.

Examples

This is a guitar.

This is a table.   ✗

Questions

This is a sausage.

Reading & Writing

Reading & Writing
Part 1

In this part, students look at the picture, read the sentence and put a tick or a cross depending on whether it is true or false.

■ Warm-up
For suggested warm-up activities see Test 1 page 16.

■ Do the test
Materials: SB pages 29 & 30

1 Ask students to turn to SB pages 29 & 30. Read the instructions together.

2 Write the example sentences on the board. Underline the key word in each, e.g. *guitar, table.* Ask students to correct the second example sentence, *(This is a) chair.*

3 Students underline the key word in the rest of the sentences and decide if the sentences are correct or not.

4 Ask students to compare answers in pairs.

5 Check answers. Students correct the false sentences. *(2 This is a skirt. 3 This is a watch. 5 This is a classroom.)*

Answer Key ➤ SB pages 29 & 30

Test 2

2   This is a shirt.   ☒

3   This is a radio.   ☒

4   This is a window.   ☑

5   This is a kitchen.   ☒

Part 2
– 5 questions –

ook and read. Write **yes** or **no**.

xamples

he woman is wearing a skirt.   _yes_

he boy on the beach is running.   _no_

uestions

The boat is green and red.   _no_

A boy is swimming in the water.   _yes_

The monkey is fishing.   _no_

A man is sleeping under a tree.   _yes_

The woman is reading a book.   _yes_

Reading & Writing

Reading & Writing
Part 2

In this part, students look at a picture, read the sentences and then write *yes* or *no*, depending on whether they are true or false.

■ Warm-up
For suggested warm-up activities see Test 1 page 18.

■ Do the test
Materials: SB page 31

1 Ask students to turn to SB page 31. Ask them some questions about the picture, e.g. *How many dogs can you see? What colour is the boat?* etc.

2 Discuss the examples together. Ask students to find evidence in the picture to justify the answers.

3 Give students some time to read the descriptions and to check that they match what is happening in the picture.

4 Ask students to compare answers in pairs.

5 Check answers. Students correct the false sentences. (1 *The boat is brown and red.* 3 *The monkey is waving.*)

Answer Key ➤ SB page 31

Test 2

Reading & Writing Part 3

In this part, students reorder letters and write words.

■ Warm-up

For suggested warm-up activities see Test 1 page 19.

■ Do the test

Materials: SB page 32

1 Ask students to turn to SB page 32. Read the instructions carefully. Explain that each dash represents a letter and that the pictures should help them.

2 Write the example on the board. Write both the jumbled letters and the word spelt correctly.

3 Give students some time to unscramble the rest of the jumbled words. Encourage them to cross out the letters after they have used them. Remind them to write only one letter in each space.

4 Ask students to compare answers in pairs.

5 Check answers. Check students have spelt the words correctly.

Answer Key ➤ SB page 32

Part 3
– 5 questions –

Look at the pictures. Look at the letters. Write the words.

Example

       d o g

Questions

1   c o w

2   s n a k e

3   s h e e p

4   l i z a r d

5   c h i c k e n

32   Test 2, Reading & Writing Part 3

Part 4

– 5 questions –

ad this. Choose a word from the box. Write the correct word next to the
mbers 1–5. There is one example.

A cat

ve in a _____house_____ , but I like playing in the **(1)** _____garden_____

h the **(2)** _____children_____ .

m black and grey and I'm not very big. I have four legs and I can run.

eep on a **(3)** _____mat_____ in the kitchen. I drink **(4)** _____milk_____

d water. I don't like cakes, but I love **(5)** _____fish_____ .

hat am I? I am a cat.

example

house	milk	apples	legs
fish	garden	children	mat

Test 2, Reading & Writing Part 4   `33`

Reading & Writing Part 4

In this part, students read a text and complete it with the missing words.

■ Warm-up

For suggested warm-up activities see Test 1 page 20.

■ Do the test

Materials: SB page 33

1 Ask students to turn to SB page 33. Read the instructions together. Ask them to say what the text is about. The picture and title will help them.

2 Discuss the example together. Ask them to cross out the word and picture in the box that was used in the example.

3 Give students some time to read the text carefully and to try to choose the best word from the box for each gap. Tell them to read the whole sentence before deciding on the best word for a gap.

4 Ask students to compare answers in pairs.

5 Check answers.

Answer Key ➤ SB page 33

Test 2

Reading & Writing Part 5

In this part, students look at a picture and then write one-word answers to questions.

■ Warm-up

For suggested warm-up activities see Test 1 page 22.

■ Do the test

Materials: SB pages 34 & 35

1 Ask students to turn to SB pages 34 & 35. Ask them to name the items in the pictures. Pre-teach any they don't know.

2 Read the instructions carefully and discuss the examples together. Ask students to point to the parts of the picture that contain the answers.

3 Give students time to read the questions and write the answers. Remind them to write only one-word answers.

4 Check answers after each section. Ask students to compare answers in pairs first. When checking the answers, make sure students have spelt the words correctly.

Answer Key ➤ SB pages 34 & 35

Part 5
– 5 questions –

Look at the pictures and read the questions. Write one-word answers.

Examples

How many people are there in the picture? _____ four

Where is the food? next to the _____ car

Questions

1 What are the children doing? _____ reading

Reading & Writing

Where are the children now?   in the _____water_____

Who has got the ball?   the _____dog_____

Where are the father and the dog sleeping?   under a _____tree_____

What is the boy doing now?   _____eating_____ a sausage

Test 2, Reading & Writing Part 5   35

Test 2

Speaking Part 1

In this part, students point to items on the scene picture.

■ Warm-up

For suggested warm-up activities see Test 1 page 24.

■ Do the test

Materials: SB page 39

1 Check students know the names of items in the scene picture, e.g. *tree, bike, basketball.*

2 Ask them some questions about the scene picture. The students should point to the items rather than describe where each item is, e.g.

This is the teacher? (Point)

Where is the bike?

Where are the fish?

etc.

Speaking Part 2

In this part, students put the object cards in various locations on the scene picture.

■ Warm-up

For suggested warm-up activities see Test 1 page 25.

■ Do the test

Materials: SB pages 37 & 39

1 Ask students to lay out the object cards on their desk.

2 Give students instructions where to put some of the object cards, e.g.

Which is the shell?

Put the shell under the tree.

Which is the hat?

Put the hat between the bike and the teacher.

Which is the duck?

Put the duck next to the school bags.

etc.

Object cards

Test 2, Speaking Parts 1–3 `39`

Speaking

■ Do the test

Materials: SB page 37

1 Ask students about the other object cards (the ones not referred to in Part 2), e.g.

What's this? (a bike)

What colour is it? (red)

Have you got a bike? (yes / no)

What colour is your bike? (blue)

Speaking Part 5

In this part, students answer personal questions.

■ Warm-up

For suggested warm-up activities see Test 1 page 27.

■ Do the test

Materials: None

1 Ask each student some questions about themselves. They can give one-word answers but encourage them to give a longer answer if they can, e.g.

How old are you? (I'm 10 years old.)

Where do you live?

What food do you like?

Speaking Part 3

In this part, students answer questions about people or things in the scene picture.

■ Warm-up

For suggested warm-up activities see Test 1 page 26.

■ Do the test

Materials: SB page 39

1 Ask students some questions about the scene picture. These questions should be ones that the students will need to answer verbally, e.g.

What is this? (bird)

What colour is it? (orange)

How many birds are there? (four)

Where are the boys? (the students point to the boys)

What are they doing? (reading)

Speaking Part 4

In this part, students answer questions about the object cards.

■ Warm-up

For suggested warm-up activities see Test 1 page 26.

Speaking frame   (Timing = 5 minutes)

What to do (use child's name throughout the test)	What to say	Answer from candidate (one word sufficient)	Back up question if necessary
Usher brings candidate into examination room	Introduces the child to the examiner: *This is …* Examiner to candidate: *Hello my name's ….*	*Hello*	
1 Examiner opens candidate booklet and shows scene to the candidate.	*Look at this. This is a playground. The children are playing basketball.* *This is the teacher.* (pointing) *Where is the bike?* *Where are the fish?*	Points to items	*Is this the bike?* (point) *Are these the fish?*
2 Point to the object cards laid out on the table.	*Look at these,* (name). *Which is the shell?* *I'm putting the shell on the teacher.* *Now you put the shell under the tree.* *Which is the hat / book?* *Now put the hat / book between the bike and the teacher.* *Which is the duck? Put the duck next to the school bags.*	Candidate points. Examiner puts shell on teacher. Candidate puts card under the tree. Candidate points and puts card between the bike and the teacher. Candidate points and places the card next to the school bags.	*Where is the tree?* <u>Under</u> *tree.* *Is this the hat / book?* (points) <u>Between</u> *the bike and the teacher.* *Is this the duck?* (points) <u>Next to</u> *the school bags.*
3 Remove the cards and point to the scene. Point to a bird. Point to boys reading. Remove scene picture.	*What's this?* *What colour is it?* *How many birds are there?* *What are the boys doing?*	*Bird* *Orange* *Four* *Reading*	*Is it a bird?* *Is it orange?* *Are there two? Three?* *Are the boys reading?*
4 Take 3 object cards not used previously. Close candidate booklet. Show bike card. Show football card. Show television card. Put away all cards.	*What's this,* (name)? *What colour is it?* *Have you got a bike?* *What colour is your bike?* *What's this?* *Do you play football?* *What's your favourite sport?* *What's this?* *Do you watch TV?* *Where is the television in your house?*	*Bike.* *Red* *Yes / no* *Blue* *Football* *Yes / no* *Swimming* *Television / TV* *Yes / no* *Living room / kitchen, etc.*	*Is it a bike?* *Is it red?* *Is it blue?* *Is it a football?* *Do you go swimming?* *Is it a television?* *Is it in the living room?*
5 Ask a few personal questions.	*Now,* (name). *How old are you?* *Where do you live?* *What food do you like?*	*10* *Name of city or town* *Pizza*	*Are you ten?* *Do you live in …* *Do you like pizza?*
	Thank you, (name). *Bye Bye.*		

Part 1
– 5 questions –

Listen and draw lines. There is one example.

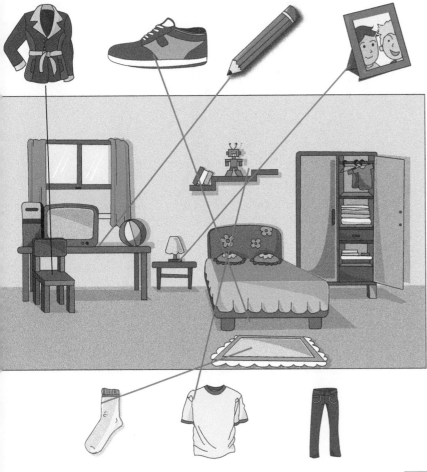

Test 3, Listening Part 1   41

Test 3

Listening Part 1

In this part, students listen and correctly position items on a picture by drawing lines.

■ Warm-up
For suggested warm-up activities see Test 1 page 8.

■ Do the test
Materials: SB page 41, Audio T3P1

1 Ask students to turn to SB page 41.
2 Point to each of the objects around the picture in turn and ask *What's this?* Get different students to answer, e.g. *It's a sock.*
3 Ask students to name all the items and colours in the picture, e.g. *They're T-shirts. They're green and red.*
4 Play the first part of the recording. Go through the example.
5 Play the rest of the recording and students draw lines to position the objects on the picture.
6 Let students listen to the recording again. Check answers.

Audioscript

R	**Look at part 1. Now look at the picture. Listen and look. There is one example.**
M	Can you see the jacket?
F	Yes, I can.
M	Put the jacket on the chair.
F	Ok. The jacket is on the chair.
R	**Can you see the line? This is an example. Now you listen and draw lines.**
	One
M	Now find the sock.
F	Where can I put it?
M	Put it on the mat.
F	Ok, the sock is on the mat now.
R	**Two**
F	And the shoe?
M	Oh, yes. Please put it under the bed.
F	Ok, I'm putting the shoe under the bed now.
M	Thank you.
R	**Three**
F	I can see a photo. Where can I put it?
M	Please put the photo on the small table near the bed.
F	On the small table?
M	Yes, please.
R	**Four**
M	There's a T-shirt.
F	Yes, I can see it.
M	Please put it next to the robot.
F	The T-shirt is next to the robot now.
R	**Five**
M	Can you find the pencil?
F	Yes! There it is.
M	Please put the pencil between the ball and the computer.
F	Ok, I'm putting it between the ball and the computer.
R	**Now listen to Part One again.**

Answer Key ➤ SB page 41

Test 3

Listening Part 2

In this part, students listen and write names or numbers.

■ Warm-up

For suggested warm-up activities see Test 1 page 10.

■ Do the test

Materials: SB pages 42 & 43, Audio T3P2.

1 Ask students to turn to SB pages 42 & 43. Explain the task and make sure students understand they should write either a name or a number.

2 Play the first part of the recording. Go through the examples.

3 Read the rest of the questions together. Ask students to guess what type of information is missing (i.e. a name or a number).

4 Play the rest of the recording and students listen and write answers.

5 Let students listen to the recording again. Check answers. Make sure the students' handwriting is legible and that they have spelt the names correctly.

Audioscript

R   **Look at the picture. Listen and write a name or a number. There are two examples.**

F   Hello. Are you the boy in the picture?

Mch   Yes. My name's Bill.

F   How do you spell it?

Mch   B-I-L-L.

F   And how old are you?

Mch   I'm seven.

F   Seven?

Mch   Yes.

Part 2
– 5 questions –

**Read the question. Listen and write a name or a number.
There are two examples.**

Examples

What's the boy's name? ——————————— Bill

How old is he? ——————————— 7

R   **Can you see the answers? Now you listen and write a name or a number.**
One

F   Is this your friend with you?

Mch   Yes it is.

F   What's her name?

Mch   Her name's Kim.

F   How do you spell that?

Mch   K-I-M.

R   Two

F   Are you in her class at school?

Mch   Yes. We're in class nine.

F   Pardon?

Mch   Class nine, and the teacher is very nice!

R   **Three**

F   Have you got a dog in your house, Bill?

Mch   No, but I've got five cats.

F   How many?

Mch   Five cats.

uestions

What is Bill's friend's name?   _____Kim_____

Which class are the children in at school?   ___9 / nine___

How many cats are in Bill's house?   ___5 / five___

What's the name of Bill's favourite cat?   ___Sam___

How many chickens has Bill's friend got?   ___15 / fifteen___

R **Four**	**Mch** Yes. They're in the garden.
F Which is your favourite cat, Bill?	**R** **Now listen to Part Two again.**
Mch Oh, Sam is my favourite. He's sleeping now.	**Answer Key ➤** SB page 43
F How do you spell the cat's name?	
Mch S-A-M.	
F That's a good name for a cat!	
R **Five**	
F Has Kim got a cat?	
Mch No. She's got chickens.	
F Chickens? How many?	
Mch She's got 15.	
F Fifteen!	

Test 3

Listening Part 3

In this part, students listen to the dialogue and tick the correct picture.

■ Warm-up

For suggested warm-up activities see Test 1 page 12.

■ Do the test

Materials: SB pages 44 & 45, Audio T3P3

1 Ask students to turn to SB pages 44 & 45. Read the questions and check students know what they mean.

2 Ask students to look at the pictures and check they know the names of the items (objects, places and colours) in them. Take this opportunity to pre-teach any words they may need to know, e.g. *orange, lemonade, watermelon*, etc.

3 Ask students to guess what each dialogue will be about.

4 Play the first part of the recording. Go through the example.

5 Play the rest of the recording and students listen and tick the correct picture.

6 Let students listen to the recording again. Check answers. Ask students to describe one or two of the pictures.

Audioscript

R **Look at the pictures. Now listen and look. There is one example.**
What's Lucy doing?

M Hello. Is Lucy reading in the bedroom?

Fch No, she isn't.

M Is she watching TV in the living room?

Fch No, she's making a cake in the kitchen.

Part 3
– 5 questions –

Listen and tick (✓) the box. There is one example.

What's Lucy doing?

A ☐   B ☐   C ✓

1   What does Ben want?

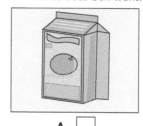 

A ☐   B ✓   C ☐

2   Which is Nick?

A ☐   B ✓   C ☐

R **Can you see the tick? Now you listen and tick the box.**
One. What does Ben want?

F Do you want some orange juice, Ben?

Mch No thanks.

F Some lemonade, then.

Mch No. Can I have some milk please?

R **Two. Which is Nick?**

M Is Nick the boy with the dog?

Mch No. That's Nick there.

M Oh yes. The boy with the cat.

Mch Yes, it's a beautiful cat.

R **Three. What's for breakfast?**

Mch Can I have fruit for breakfast, please?

F Yes, we've got grapes, oranges, bananas and watermelon.

Mch Can I have grapes and watermelon, please?

F Yes, here you are.

R **Four. Where is Ann's pen?**

Fch Mum, where's my new pen? Have you got it?

What's for breakfast?

 A ✓

 B ☐

 C ☐

Where is Ann's pen?

 A ☐

 B ☐

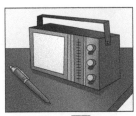 C ✓

Which book would Sam like?

 A ☐

 B ☐

 C ✓

Test 3, Listening Part 3   45

F	No. Look on your desk Ann!
Fch	It isn't there and it isn't in my school bag.
F	Oh, look. There it is. Next to the radio!
R	**Five. Which book would Sam like?**
Mch	Mum, can I have a book about animals?
F	Yes, would you like this one with snakes? Or one with lizards?
Mch	No, I don't like them.
F	What about this one with monkeys. Would you like it?

Mch	Yes. It's great!
R	**Now listen to Part Three again.**

Answer Key ➤ SB pages 44 & 45

Test 3

Listening Part 4

In this part, the students listen and colour items in a picture.

■ Warm-up

For suggested warm-up activities see Test 1 page 14.

■ Do the test

Materials: SB page 46, Audio T3P4, coloured pencils

1 Ask students to turn to SB page 46. Read the instructions.
2 Check students have all the colours they will need.
3 Check students know the name of the items in the picture. Ask them to predict what colour they think each item will be.
4 Play the first part of the recording. Go through the example.
5 Play the rest of the recording and students listen and colour the picture.
6 Let students listen to the recording again. Check answers.

Audioscript

R	**Look at the picture. Listen and look. There is one example.**
M	Can you see the fish in the water?
Fch	Yes, I can.
M	Well, colour that fish red.
Fch	Pardon?
M	Colour the fish in the water. Colour it red.
R	**Can you see the red fish in the water? This is an example. Now you listen and colour.**
	One
M	Look at the fish on the boat.
Fch	Can I colour it?
M	Yes. Colour it green
Fch	Ok. A green fish on the boat.
R	**Two**
M	Now find the fish on the woman's hat.

Part 4
– 5 questions –

Listen and colour. There is one example.

46 Test 3, Listening Part 4

Fch	Where?
M	The fish on the hat. Colour it yellow.
Fch	Yellow?
M	Yes.
R	**Three**
M	Can you see the boy under the umbrella? He's wearing a T-shirt with a fish on it.
Fch	Oh. Yes!
M	Good. Colour the fish on his T-shirt blue.
Fch	Ok, a blue fish. That's funny!
R	**Four**
M	Now find the girl's bag.
Fch	The girl's bag? Ok. I can see it.

M	There's a fish on it. Colour that fish brown.
Fch	Brown?
M	Yes, please.
R	**Five**
M	Look at the boys. They're playing with a ball.
Fch	There's a fish on it. Can I colour it?
M	Yes. Colour it orange.
Fch	Ok. The fish on the ball is orange.
M	I like this picture now.
R	**Now listen to Part Four again.**

Answer Key ➤ SB page 46

Part 1
– 5 questions –

ok and read. Put a tick (✓) or a cross (X) in the box.

ere are two examples.

amples

This is a flower. | ✓

This is a television. | X

uestions

This is an eraser. | X

Reading & Writing

Reading & Writing
Part 1

In this part, students look at the picture, read the sentence and put a tick or a cross depending on whether it is true or false.

■ Warm-up

For suggested warm-up activities see Test 1 page 16.

■ Do the test

Materials: SB pages 47 & 48

1 Ask students to turn to SB pages 47 & 48. Read the instructions together.

2 Write the example sentences on the board. Underline the key word in each, e.g. *flower, television*. Ask students to correct the second example sentence, e.g. *(This is a) telephone*.

3 Students underline the key word in the rest of the sentences and decide if the sentences are correct or not.

4 Ask students to compare answers in pairs.

5 Check answers. Students correct the false sentences. *(1 This is a ruler. 3 This is an apple. 5 This is a lizard.)*

Answer Key ➤ SB pages 47 & 48

Test 3

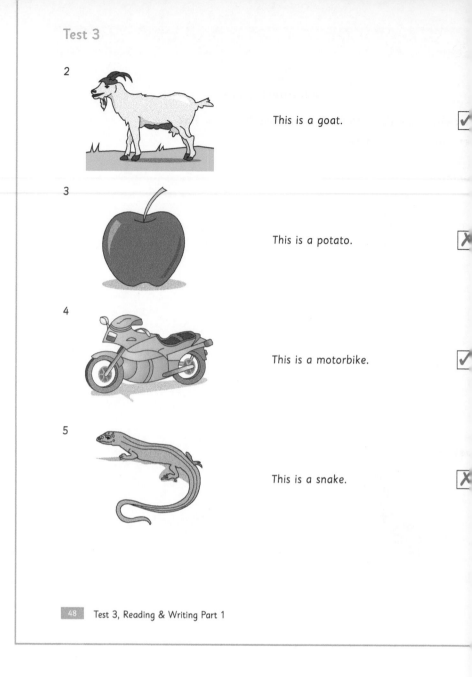

2

This is a goat. ✓

3

This is a potato. ✗

4

This is a motorbike. ✓

5

This is a snake. ✗

Part 2
– 5 questions –

ok and read. Write **yes** or **no**.

xamples

There are two orange trees.	_yes_
The birds are flying.	_no_

uestions

The boy has got four oranges.	_no_
The apples on the tree are green.	_no_
There are watermelons in a blue bag.	_yes_
A lizard is sleeping under the pear tree.	_yes_
A girl is picking up a tomato.	_yes_

Test 3, Reading & Writing Part 2   49

Reading & Writing

Reading & Writing Part 2

In this part, students look at a picture, read the sentences and then write *yes* or *no*, depending on whether they are true or false.

■ Warm-up
For suggested warm-up activities see Test 1 page 18.

■ Do the test
Materials: SB page 49

1 Ask students to turn to SB page 49. Ask them some questions about the picture, e.g. *How many watermelons can you see? What colour is the bag?* etc.

2 Discuss the examples together. Ask students to find evidence in the picture to justify the answers.

3 Give students some time to read the descriptions and to check that they match what is happening in the picture.

4 Ask students to compare answers in pairs.

5 Check answers. Students correct the false sentences. (1 *The boy has got three oranges.* 2 *The apples on the tree are red.*)

Answer Key ➤ SB page 49

Test 3

Reading & Writing
Part 3

In this part, students reorder letters and write words.

■ Warm-up

For suggested warm-up activities see Test 1 page 19.

■ Do the test

Materials: SB page 50

1 Ask students to turn to SB page 50. Read the instructions carefully. Explain that each dash represents a letter and that the pictures should help them.

2 Write the example on the board. Write both the jumbled letters and the word spelt correctly.

3 Give students some time to unscramble the rest of the jumbled words. Encourage them to cross out the letters after they have used them. Remind them to write only one letter in each space.

4 Ask students to compare answers in pairs.

5 Check answers. Check students have spelt the words correctly.

Answer Key ➤ SB page 50

Part 3
– 5 questions –

Look at the pictures. Look at the letters. Write the words.

Example

 chips

Questions

1 cake

2 meat

3 onion

4 banana

5 pineapple

50   Test 3, Reading & Writing Part 3

Part 4
– 5 questions –

ead this. Choose a word from the box. Write the correct word next to the
mbers 1–5. There is one example.

A park

m big with a lot of _____trees_____ and (1) _____flowers_____ .
e (2) _____children_____ run and play in me. They can ride (3) _____bikes_____
d fly kites in one.

my trees there are black, blue and green (4) _____birds_____ but there are
elephants or hippos.

pen in the (5) _____morning_____ and I close in the evening.

at am I? I am a park.

example			
trees	birds	morning	flowers
chicken	bikes	shop	children

Test 3, Reading & Writing Part 4   **51**

Reading & Writing
Part 4

In this part, students read a text
and complete it with the missing
words.

■ Warm-up

For suggested warm-up activities
see Test 1 page 20.

■ Do the test

Materials: SB page 51

1 Ask students to turn to SB
   page 51. Read the instructions
   together. Ask them to say what
   the text is about. The picture
   and title will help them.

2 Discuss the example together.
   Ask them to cross out the
   word and picture in the box
   that was used in the example.

3 Give students some time to
   read the text carefully and to
   try to choose the best word
   from the box for each gap.
   Tell them to read the whole
   sentence before deciding on
   the best word for a gap.

4 Ask students to compare
   answers in pairs.

5 Check answers.

Answer Key ➤ SB page 51

Test 3

Reading & Writing Part 5

In this part, students look at a picture and then write one-word answers to questions.

■ Warm-up
For suggested warm-up activities see Test 1 page 22.

■ Do the test
Materials: SB pages 52 & 53

1 Ask students to turn to SB pages 52 & 53. Ask them to name the items in the pictures. Pre-teach any they don't know.

2 Read the instructions carefully and discuss the examples together. Ask students to point to the parts of the picture that contain the answers.

3 Give students time to read the questions and write the answers. Remind them to write only one-word answers.

4 Check answers after each section. Ask students to compare answers in pairs first. When checking the answers, make sure students have spelt the words correctly.

Answer Key ➤ SB pages 52 & 53

Part 5
– 5 questions –

Look at the pictures and read the questions. Write one-word answers.

Examples

What is the teacher wearing?   a _____skirt_____

How many children are there?   _____five_____

Questions

1   What is the boy with the red T-shirt doing?   _____kicking_____ a b

Who is holding the ball?   the _____teacher_____

What are the children looking at?   a _____plane_____

Where are the children now?   in the _____classroom_____

What is the teacher doing?   _____pointing_____ to the board

Test 3

Speaking Part 1

In this part, students point to items on the scene picture.

■ Warm-up

For suggested warm-up activities see Test 1 page 24.

■ Do the test

Materials: SB page 57

1 Ask students to turn to SB page 57.
2 Check students know the names of items in the scene picture, e.g. *sun, crocodile.*
3 Ask them some questions about the scene picture. The students should point to the items rather than describe where each item is, e.g.

Where is the crocodile?

Where are the bags?

Where is the monkey?

etc.

Speaking Part 2

In this part, students put the object cards in various locations on the scene picture.

■ Warm-up

For suggested warm-up activities see Test 1 page 25.

■ Do the test

Materials: SB pages 55 & 57

1 Ask students to prepare the object cards on page 55 and then turn to page 57 in their SB.
2 Ask students to lay out the object cards on their desk.
3 Give students instructions where to put some of the object cards, e.g.

Which is the box?

Put the box behind the woman.

Object cards

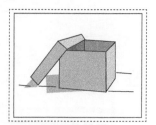

Test 3, Speaking Parts 2 & 4   55

Which is the helicopter?

Put the helicopter in front of the ball.

Which is the camera?

Put the camera between the birds and the sun.

etc.

Test 3, Speaking Parts 1–3   57

■ Do the test

Materials: SB page 55

1 Ask students to lay the object cards face up on the table.

2 Ask them questions about the other object cards (the ones not referred to in Part 2), e.g.

What are these? (grapes)

Do you like grapes? (yes / no)

What's your favourite fruit? (bananas, etc.)

Speaking Part 5

In this part, students answer personal questions.

■ Warm-up

For suggested warm-up activities see Test 1 page 27.

■ Do the test

Materials: none

1 Ask each student some questions about themselves. They can give one-word answers but encourage them to give a longer answer if they can, e.g.

How old are you? (I'm 9 years old.)

What's your name? (Lisa)

What's your mother's name? (Ann)

Has she got brown eyes? (yes / no)

How many people live in your house / flat? (four)

Speaking Part 3

In this part, students answer questions about people or things in the scene picture.

■ Warm-up

For suggested warm-up activities see Test 1 page 26.

■ Do the test

Materials: SB page 57

1 Ask students to turn to SB page 57.

2 Ask students some questions about the scene picture. These questions should be ones that the students will need to answer verbally, e.g.

What's this? (a boat)

What colour is it? (red)

How many boats are there? (three)

Where are the boys? (the students point to the boys)

What are they doing? (They're eating ice cream)

Speaking Part 4

In this part, students answer questions about the object cards.

■ Warm-up

For suggested warm-up activities see Test 1 page 26.

Speaking frame   (Timing = 5 minutes)

What to do (use child's name throughout the test)	What to say	Answer from candidate (one word sufficient)	Back up question if necessary
Usher brings candidate into examination room	Introduces the child to the examiner: *This is ...* Examiner to candidate: *Hello my name's ...*	*Hello*	
1 Examiner opens candidate booklet and shows scene to the candidate.	*Look at this. This is the sea. There are some people in the water.* *This is an umbrella.* (pointing) *Where is the crocodile?* *Where are the bags?*	Points to items	*Is this the crocodile?* (point) *Are these the bags?*
2 Point to the object cards laid out on the table.	*Look at these,* (name). *Which is the box?* *I'm putting the box on the monkey.* *Now you put the box behind the woman.* *Which is the helicopter / piano?* *Now put the helicopter / piano in front of the ball.* *Which is the camera / computer?* *Put the camera / computer between the birds and the sun.*	Candidate points. Examiner puts box on the monkey. Candidate puts card behind the woman. Candidate points and puts card in front of the ball. Candidate points and places the card between the birds and the sun	*Where is the woman?* <u>Behind</u> *the woman.* *Is this the helicopter / piano?* (points) <u>In front of</u> *the ball.* *Is this the helicopter / computer?* (points) <u>Between</u> *the birds and the sun.*
3 Remove the cards and point to the scene. Point to a boat. Point to boys eating ice cream. Remove picture.	*What's this?* *What colour is it?* *How many boats are there?* *What are the boys doing?*	Boat Red Three Eating (ice cream)	*Is it a boat?* *Is it green? Red?* *Are there three? Four?* *Are the boys eating?*
4 Take 3 object cards not used previously. Close candidate booklet. Show grapes card. Show snake card. Show chips / French fries card. Put away all cards.	*What are these* (name)? *Do you like grapes?* *What's your favourite fruit?* *What's this?* *Do you like snakes?* *What animal do you like?* *What are these?* *Do you eat chips for lunch?* *Where do you have breakfast?*	Grapes Yes / no Bananas Snake Yes / no Dog Chips Yes / no Kitchen	*Are they grapes?* *Do you like bananas?* *Is it a snake?* *Do you like dogs?* *Are they chips?* *Do you have breakfast in the kitchen?*
5 Ask a few personal questions.	*Now,* (name). *What's your mother's / father's name?* *Has he / she got blue or brown eyes?* *How many people live in your house / flat?*	Ann / Peter Blue 4	*Is your father's name ...?* *Has he / she got blue eyes?* *Do four people live in your house / flat?*
	Thank you, (name). *Bye Bye.*		

Part 1
– 5 questions –

Listen and draw lines. There is one example.

Test 4, Listening Part 1   59

Test 4

Listening Part 1

In this part, students listen and correctly position items on a picture by drawing lines.

■ Warm-up

For suggested warm-up activities see Test 1 page 8.

■ Do the test

Materials: SB page 59, Audio T4P1

1 Ask students to turn to SB page 59.
2 Point to each of the objects around the picture in turn and ask *What's this?* Get different students to answer, e.g. *It's a lizard.*
3 Ask students to name all the items and colours in the picture, e.g. *It's a cat. It's white.*
4 Play the first part of the recording. Go through the example.
5 Play the rest of the recording and students draw lines to position the objects on the picture.
6 Let students listen to the recording again. Check answers.

Audioscript

R	**Now look at the picture. Listen and look. There is one example.**
F	Can you see the goat?
M	Yes.
F	Well, put it next to the chicken
M	OK.
R	**Can you see the line? This is an example. Now you listen and draw lines. One**
F	Now find the snake.
M	I can see it.
F	Please put it under the horse.
M	The snake is under the horse. OK.
R	**Two**
F	Put the mouse in front of the woman.
M	Sorry. Put the mouse where?
F	Put it in front of the woman.
M	OK.
R	**Three**
F	Now find the duck.
M	OK. I can see it.
F	Put the duck between the boy and the dog.
M	Ok, it's there now.
R	**Four**
F	Right, can you see the fish?
M	Yes, can I put it in the water?
F	Yes. Put the fish in the water now.
M	OK.
R	**Five**
F	And now the sheep. Can you see it?
M	Yes. There it is.
F	Can you put the sheep behind the girl?
M	Ok. I'm putting it behind the girl now.
R	**Now listen to Part One again.**

Answer Key ➤ SB page 59

Test 4

Listening Part 2

In this part, students listen and write names or numbers.

■ Warm-up

For suggested warm-up activities see Test 1 page 10.

■ Do the test

Materials: SB pages 60 & 61, Audio T4P2

1 Ask students to turn to SB pages 60 & 61. Explain the task and make sure students understand they should write either a name or a number.

2 Play the first part of the recording. Go through the examples.

3 Read the rest of the questions together. Ask students to guess what type of information is missing (i.e. a name or a number).

4 Play the rest of the recording and students listen and write answers.

5 Let students listen to the recording again. Check answers. Make sure the students' handwriting is legible and that they have spelt the names correctly.

Audioscript

R	**Look at the picture. Listen and write a name or a number. There are two examples.**
F	Hello. What's your name?
Mch	My name's Sam.
F	Can you spell Sam, please?
Mch	Yes. It's S-A-M.
F	And how old are you?
Mch	I'm ten!
F	Wow! Ten.
Mch	Yes, I'm very big now.

Part 2
– 5 questions –

Read the question. Listen and write a name or a number.
There are two examples.

Examples

What's the boy's name? _____ Sam

How old is he? _____ 10

R	**Can you see the answers? Now you listen and write a name or a number.**
	One
Mch	Look this is my mum in the photo.
F	Oh. What's her name?
Mch	Her name's Jill.
F	Can you spell that, please?
Mch	J-I-L-L.
F	Thanks.
R	**Two**
F	And is this a photo of your grandfather?

Mch	Yes. His name's Ben.
F	Can you spell it?
Mch	Yes, I can. It's B-E-N.
R	**Three**
Mch	My sister is in this photo.
F	She's small. How old is she?
Mch	She's one now.
F	One! Can she walk?
Mch	Yes, she can.
R	**Four**
F	Have you got a brother too, Sam?
Mch	Yes, I've got three.

estions

What is Sam's mum's name? _____ Jill _____

What's the name of Sam's grandfather? _____ Ben _____

How old is Sam's sister? _____ 1 / one _____

How many brothers has Sam got? _____ 3 / three _____

Where does Sam go to school? _____ Black _____ Wall School

F	Three?
Mch	Yes. We're a big family!
R	**Five**
Mch1	Look. Here's a picture of my school.
F 2	Oh! Where do you go to school?
Mch1	I go to Black Wall school.
F 2	Can you spell that?
Mch1	Yes I can. It's B-L-A-C-K.
F 1	Right. Thanks.
R	**Now listen to Part Two again.**

Answer Key ➤ SB page 61

Listening Part 3

In this part, students listen to the dialogue and tick the correct picture.

■ Warm-up

For suggested warm-up activities see Test 1 page 12.

■ Do the test

Materials: SB pages 62 & 63, Audio T4P3

1 Ask students to turn to SB pages 62 & 63. Read the questions and check students know what they mean.

2 Ask students to look at the pictures and check they know the names of the items (objects, places and colours) in them. Take this opportunity to pre-teach any words they may need to know, e.g. *jacket, computer, garden*, etc.

3 Ask students to guess what each dialogue will be about.

4 Play the first part of the recording. Go through the example.

5 Play the rest of the recording and students listen and tick the correct picture.

6 Let students listen to the recording again. Check answers. Ask students to describe one or two of the pictures.

Audioscript

R **Look at the pictures. Now listen and look. There is one example.**
Which is Tom's brother?

Fch Tom, is that boy with the red trousers your brother?

Mch No, that's my friend.

Fch Is your brother the boy with the green T-shirt?

Mch No. he's wearing a yellow one today and a jacket.

Part 3
– 5 questions –

Listen and tick (✓) the box. There is one example.

Which is Tom's brother?

A ✓   B ☐   C ☐

1 What does Pat like doing?

A ☐   B ✓   C ☐

2 Which is Tony's house?

A ☐   B ☐   C ✓

62   Test 4, Listening Part 3

R **Can you see the tick? Now you listen and tick the box.**
One. What does Pat like doing?

M Do you like dancing, Pat?

Fch No, but my sister enjoys it.

M I like playing with the computer.

Fch I don't. I love swimming.

R **Two. Which is Tony's house?**

M Is that Tony's house with the trees?

Mch No, that's Ben's house.

M Is Tony's the one with the car in front of it?

Mch No, look! His house has got a garden with flowers in it.

R **Three. What's Lucy's dad doing?**

M Hello, Lucy. Is your dad making lunch now?

Fch No, he's in the living room.

M Is he painting the room?

Fch No, he's reading a book.

R **Four. What animals has Sue's grandmother got?**

F Has your grandmother got chickens, Sue?

What's Lucy's dad doing?

A ☑

B ☐

C ☐

What animals has Sue's grandmother got?

A ☐

B ☐

C ☑

Where is Kim's dad?

A ☑

B ☐

C ☐

Test 4, Listening Part 3   63

Fch	No, not now.
F	Has she got sheep then?
Fch	No, but she has got some cows.
R	**Five. Where is Kim's dad?**
Mch	Is that your dad, Kim? The man in the car?
Fch	No. there he is, next to his lorry.
Mch	Yes, I see him.
Fch	And my mum is on the big motorbike!
R	**Now listen to Part Three again.**

Answer Key ➤ SB pages 62 & 63

Test 4

Listening Part 4

In this part, the students listen and colour items in a picture.

■ Warm-up

For suggested warm-up activities see Test 1 page 14.

■ Do the test

Materials: SB page 64, Audio T4P4, coloured pencils

1 Ask students to turn to SB page 64. Read the instructions.

2 Check students have all the colours they will need.

3 Check students know the name of the items in the picture. Ask them to predict what colour they think each item will be.

4 Play the first part of the recording. Go through the example.

5 Play the rest of the recording and students listen and colour the picture.

6 Let students listen to the recording again. Check answers.

Audioscript

R **Look at the picture. Listen and look. There is one example.**

F Can you see the robots?

Mch Mmm. Yes. One is on the desk next to the computer.

F Yes, well. Colour that robot brown.

Mch Pardon?

F The robot on the desk. Colour it brown.

R **Can you see the brown robot on the desk? This is an example. Now you listen and colour. One**

F Right. There's a robot between the flowers and the photo. Can you see it?

Mch Yes, I can see it. Can I colour it pink?

F Ok.

Mch The robot between the photo and the flowers is pink now.

R **Two**

Mch Look at that robot on the jeans!

Part 4
– 5 questions –

Listen and colour. There is one example.

F Oh, yes. Can you colour it yellow?

Mch Colour the robot on the jeans yellow?

F Yes. Thank you.

R **Three**

Mch What can I colour now?

F Well, can you see the picture on the wall?

Mch Oh, yes. It's a picture of a robot!

F Colour that robot red.

Mch The robot in the picture on the wall is red now.

R **Four**

Mch There's a robot on the mat too!

F Yes, there is.

Mch Can I colour it green?

F Yes, the robot on the mat. Colour it green.

R **Five**

F Look at the robot on the bed.

Mch Oh yes. It's sleeping. Can I colour it?

F What's your favourite colour?

Mch It's blue. Can I do it that colour?

F Yes, please. Colour the robot on the bed blue.

Mch That's a nice picture now.

R **Now listen to Part Four again.**

Answer Key ➤ SB page 64

Part 1
– 5 questions –

ok and read. Put a tick (✓) or a cross (X) in the box.

ere are two examples.

amples

This is a ball.

This is a horse.

uestions

This is a bus.

Reading & Writing

Reading & Writing
Part 1

In this part, students look at the picture, read the sentence and put a tick or a cross depending on whether it is true or false.

■ Warm-up
For suggested warm-up activities see Test 1 page 16.

■ Do the test
Materials: SB pages 65 & 66

1 Ask students to turn to SB pages 65 & 66. Read the instructions together.

2 Write the example sentences on the board. Underline the key word in each, e.g. *ball, horse.* Ask students to correct the second example sentence, e.g. *This is a cow.*

3 Students underline the key word in the rest of the sentences and decide if the sentences are correct or not.

4 Ask students to compare answers in pairs.

5 Check answers. Students correct the false sentences. (1 *This is a car.* 2 *This is a dog.* 5 *This is a piano.*)

Answer Key ➤ SB pages 65 & 66

Test 4

2

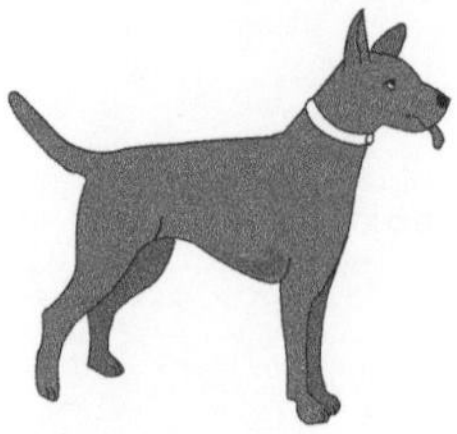

This is a cat. ☒

3

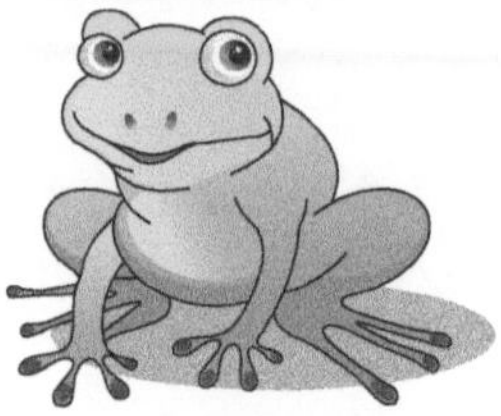

This is a frog. ☑

4

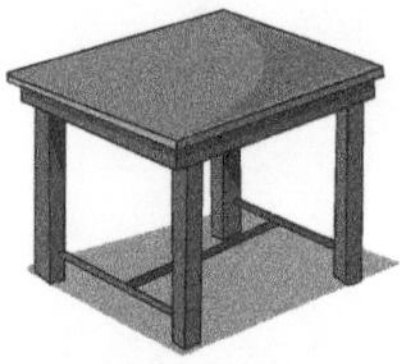

This is a table. ☑

5

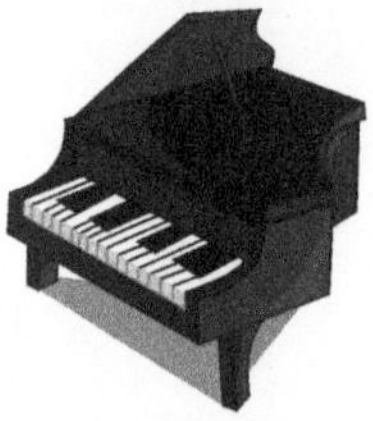

This is a guitar. ☒

Part 2
– 5 questions –

ook and read. Write **yes** or **no**.

Examples

There is a mirror on the wall.	_yes_
The window is open.	_no_

Questions

The girl is playing with a boat.	_yes_
There is a blue bird flying.	_no_
The door of the cupboard is closed.	_no_
The mat is red and blue.	_yes_
The boy is washing his hair.	_no_

Test 4, Reading & Writing Part 2   67

Reading & Writing

Reading & Writing
Part 2

In this part, students look at a picture, read the sentences and then write *yes* or *no*, depending on whether they are true or false.

■ Warm-up

For suggested warm-up activities see Test 1 page 18.

■ Do the test

Materials: SB page 67

1 Ask students to turn to SB page 67. Ask them some questions about the picture, e.g. *How many children can you see? What colour is the mat?* etc.

2 Discuss the examples together. Ask students to find evidence in the picture to justify the answers.

3 Give students some time to read the descriptions and to check that they match what is happening in the picture.

4 Ask students to compare answers in pairs.

5 Check answers. Students correct the false sentences. (*2 There is a red bird sitting. 3 The door of the cupboard is open. 5 The boy is washing his face.*)

Answer Key ➤ SB page 67

Test 4

Reading & Writing Part 3

In this part, students reorder letters and write words.

■ Warm-up

For suggested warm-up activities see Test 1 page 19.

■ Do the test

Materials: SB page 68

1 Ask students to turn to SB page 68. Read the instructions carefully. Explain that each dash represents a letter and that the pictures should help them.

2 Write the example on the board. Write both the jumbled letters and the word spelt correctly.

3 Give students some time to unscramble the rest of the jumbled words. Encourage them to cross out the letters after they have used them. Remind them to write only one letter in each space.

4 Ask students to compare answers in pairs.

5 Check answers. Check students have spelt the words correctly.

Answer Key ➤ SB page 68

Part 3
– 5 questions –

Look at the pictures. Look at the letters. Write the words.

Example

t e n n i s

Questions

1
fishing

2
football

3
swimming

4
baseball

5
badminton

68   Test 4, Reading & Writing Part 3

Part 4
– 5 questions –

ad this. Choose a word from the box. Write the correct word next to the
mbers 1–5. There is one example.

A television

u can find me in a _____ house _____ . I am in the bedroom, kitchen or the

__ living room __ . I am on a **(2)** _____ table _____ or a cupboard.

person sits on an **(3)** _____ armchair _____ in front of me. People can put a

mp or a **(4)** _____ clock _____ on me.

__ children __ like watching me and can learn from me.

at am I? I am a television.

example

house	park	cat	clock
table	armchair	living room	children

Reading & Writing

Reading & Writing Part 4

In this part, students read a text and complete it with the missing words.

■ Warm-up
For suggested warm-up activities see Test 1 page 20.

■ Do the test
Materials: SB page 69

1 Ask students to turn to SB page 69. Read the instructions together. Ask them to say what the text is about. The picture and title will help them.

2 Discuss the example together. Ask them to cross out the word and picture in the box that was used in the example.

3 Give students some time to read the text carefully and to try to choose the best word from the box for each gap. Tell them to read the whole sentence before deciding on the best word for a gap.

4 Ask students to compare answers in pairs.

5 Check answers.

Answer Key ➤ SB page 69

Test 4

Reading & Writing Part 5

In this part, students look at a picture and then write one-word answers to questions.

■ Warm-up

For suggested warm-up activities see Test 1 page 22.

■ Do the test

Materials: SB pages 70 & 71

1 Ask students to turn to SB pages 70 & 71. Ask them to name the items in the pictures. Pre-teach any they don't know.

2 Read the instructions carefully and discuss the examples together. Ask students to point to the parts of the picture that contain the answers.

3 Give students time to read the questions and write the answers. Remind them to write only one-word answers.

4 Check answers after each section. Ask students to compare answers in pairs first. When checking the answers, make sure students have spelt the words correctly.

Answer Key ➤ SB pages 70 & 71

Part 5
– 5 questions –

Look at the pictures and read the questions. Write one-word answers.

Examples

Where are the fish?	in the _____ water
How many fish are there?	_____ six

Questions

1	What is the boy holding?	a _____ kite

70   Test 4, Reading & Writing Part 5

What is the dog doing?   it's ___swimming___

What has the girl got?   a ___bag___

Where is the dog?   under a ___tree___

How many birds are there on the trees?   ___four___

Test 4

Speaking Part 1

In this part, students point to items on the scene picture.

■ Warm-up

For suggested warm-up activities see Test 1 page 24.

■ Do the test

Materials: SB page 75

1 Ask students to turn to SB page 75.
2 Check students know the names of items in the scene picture, e.g. *tiger, snake*.
3 Ask them some questions about the scene picture. The students should point to the items rather than describe where each item is, e.g.

Where is the tiger?

Where are the girls?

Where is the snake?

etc.

Speaking Part 2

In this part, students put the object cards in various locations on the scene picture.

■ Warm-up

For suggested warm-up activities see Test 1 page 25.

■ Do the test

Materials: SB pages 73 & 75

1 Ask students to prepare the object cards on page 73 and then turn to page 75 in their SB.
2 Ask students to lay out the object cards on their desk.
3 Give students instructions where to put some of the object cards, e.g.

Which is the carrot?

Put the carrot under the tiger.

Which is the book?

Object cards

Put the book between the bikes.

Which is the pencil?

Put the pencil under the bird.

Which is the sock?

Put the sock between the girl and the bird.

etc.

■ Do the test

Materials: SB page 73

1 Ask students to lay the object cards face up on the table.

2 Ask them questions about the other object cards (the ones not referred to in Part 2), e.g.

What are these? (eyes)

Have you got blue eyes? (yes / no)

What's your favourite colour? (red, etc.)

Speaking Part 5

In this part, students answer personal questions.

■ Warm-up

For suggested warm-up activities see Test 1 page 27.

■ Do the test

Materials: none

1 Ask each student some questions about themselves. They can give one-word answers but encourage them to give a longer answer if they can, e.g.

What's your name? (Paul)

How old are you? (I'm 9 years old.)

Is your school big or small? (big)

How many teachers have you got? (four)

Speaking Part 3

In this part, students answer questions about people or things in the scene picture.

■ Warm-up

For suggested warm-up activities see Test 1 page 26.

■ Do the test

Materials: SB page 75

1 Ask students to turn to SB page 75.

2 Ask students some questions about the scene picture. These questions should be ones that the students will need to answer verbally, e.g.

What's this? (sun)

What colour is it? (yellow)

How many suns are there? (one)

Where are the girls? (the students point to the girls)

What are they doing? (they're singing)

Speaking Part 4

In this part, students answer questions about the object cards.

■ Warm-up

For suggested warm-up activities see Test 1 page 26.

Test 4

Speaking frame (Timing = 5 minutes)

What to do (use child's name throughout the test)	What to say	Answer from candidate (one word sufficient)	Back up question if necessary
Usher brings candidate into examination room	Introduces the child to the examiner: *This is …* Examiner to candidate: *Hello my name's …*	*Hello*	
1 Examiner opens candidate booklet and shows scene to the candidate.	*Look at this. This is a park. There are some children playing.* *This is a tree. (pointing)* *Where is the tiger?* *Where are the girls?*	*Points to items*	*Is this the tiger? (point)* *Are these the girls?*
2 Point to the object cards laid out on the table.	*Look at these, (name).* *Which is the carrot?* *I'm putting the carrot next to the kite.* *Now you put the carrot under the tiger.* *Which is the book?* *Now put the book between the bikes.* *Which is the pencil / dress?* *Put the pencil / dress under the bird.*	Candidate points. Examiner puts carrot next to the kite. Candidate puts card under the tiger. Candidate points and puts card between the bikes. Candidate points and places the card under the bird.	*Where is the tiger?* <u>Under</u> the tiger. *Is this the book? (points)* <u>Between</u> the bikes. *Is this the pencil / dress? (points)* <u>Under</u> the bird.
3 Remove the cards and point to the scene. Point to the sun. Point to girls singing. Remove scene picture.	*What's this?* *What colour is it?* *How many suns are there?* *What are the girls doing?*	*Sun* *Yellow* *One* *Singing*	*Is it a coconut?* *Is it brown? Yellow?* *Are there four? Five?* *Are the girls singing?*
4 Take 3 object cards not used previously. Close candidate booklet. Show eyes card. Show socks card. Show school bag card. Put away all cards.	*What are these? (name)* *Have you got blue eyes?* *What's your favourite colour?* *What are these?* *Are you wearing socks today?* *What do you like wearing?* *What's this?* *Have you got a school bag?* *Is your / this school bag new or old?*	*Eyes* *Yes / no* *Red* *Socks* *Yes / no* *Jeans* *School bag* *Yes / no* *New*	*Are they eyes?* *Do you like red?* *Are they socks?* *Do you like jeans?* *Is it a school bag?* *Is your / this school bag old?*
5 Ask a few personal questions.	*Now, (name). How old are you?* *Is your school big or small?* *How many teachers have you got?*	*9* *Big* *4*	*Are you 9?* *Is your school big?* *Have you got four teachers?*
	Thank you, (name). *Bye Bye.*		

Part 1
– 5 questions –

Listen and draw lines. There is one example.

Test 5, Listening Part 1   77

Listening

Audioscript

R	**Now look at the picture. Listen and look. There is one example.**
M	Can you see the egg?
F	Sorry, what?
M	The egg. Please put it on the bird's head.
F	Ok, it's on the bird's head now.
R	**Can you see the line? This is an example. Now you listen and draw lines.** **One**
M	Now, Can you put the cake in the dog's mouth?
F	Pardon?
M	Please put the cake in the dog's mouth.
F	Right!
R	**Two**
M	Now the jeans. Put them between the girls.
F	Sorry. Put the jeans where?
M	Put them between the girls.
F	OK.
R	**Three**
F	I can see a skirt! Where can I put it?
M	Put the skirt next to the woman.
F	Next to the woman.
M	Yes, please.
R	**Four**
M	Look at the boy with an ice cream!
F	OK.
M	Put the banana in front of him.
F	Yes, OK. I'm putting the banana in front of him.
R	**Five**
M	And can you find the potato?
F	Yes. There it is.
M	Please put it under the ball.
F	Ok. The potato is under the ball.
M	Thanks.
R	**Now listen to Part One again.**

Answer Key ➤ SB page 77

Test 5

Listening Part 1

In this part, students listen and correctly position items on a picture by drawing lines.

■ Warm-up

For suggested warm-up activities see Test 1 page 8.

■ Do the test

Materials: SB page 77, Audio T5P1

1 Ask students to turn to SB page 77.

2 Point to each of the objects around the picture in turn and ask *What's this?* Get different students to answer, e.g. *It's an egg.*

3 Ask students to name all the items and colours in the picture, e.g. *They're girls. They're sitting.*

4 Play the first part of the recording. Go through the example.

5 Play the rest of the recording and students draw lines to position the objects on the picture.

6 Let students listen to the recording again. Check answers.

Test 5

Listening Part 2

In this part, students listen and write names or numbers.

■ Warm-up

For suggested warm-up activities see Test 1 page 10.

■ Do the test

Materials: SB pages 78 & 79, Audio T5P2

1 Ask students to turn to SB pages 78 & 79. Explain the task and make sure students understand they should write either a name or a number.

2 Play the first part of the recording. Go through the examples.

3 Read the rest of the questions together. Ask students to guess what type of information is missing (i.e. a name or a number).

4 Play the rest of the recording and students listen and write answers.

5 Let students listen to the recording again. Check answers. Make sure the students' handwriting is legible and that they have spelt the names correctly.

Audioscript

R **Look at the picture. Listen and write a name or a number. There are two examples.**

Fch Hello! This is my dog.

M What's the dog's name?

Fch It's Tom.

M Oh. Can you spell that, please?

Fch Yes! It's T-O-M.

M Thanks. How old is Tom?

Fch He's four.

M Four?

Fch That's right.

Part 2
– 5 questions –

Read the question. Listen and write a name or a number.
There are two examples.

Examples

What is the dog's name?   Tom

How old is it?   4

R **Can you see the answers? Now you listen and write a name or a number.**
One

M And what's your name?

Fch My name's Grace.

M Can you spell it, please?

Fch Yes, it's G-R-A-C-E.

M Good!

R **Two**

M Do you go to school?

Fch Yes. I go to Bird House school.

M Oh. How do you spell that?

Fch It's B-I-R-D.

R **Three**

M Who sits next to you in class?

Fch My friend Alex.

M Is that a boy or a girl?

Fch It's a girl. She spells it A-L-E-X.

R **Four**

M Does Alex have a dog too?

Fch No, she doesn't but she has two goats!

M Two goats?

Fch Yes. They live in a small house in the garden.

Questions

What is the girl's name? _____ Grace _____

What's the name of her school? ____ Bird ____ House School

Who does she sit next to? _____ Alex _____

How many goats has she got? ____ 2 / two ____

How many hippos are in the book? ____ 8 / eight ____

R	**Five**
Fch	We're reading a book at school. There's a family of hippos in it.
M	Oh. How many hippos are there?
Fch	Eight!
M	Eight!
Fch	Yes, it's a big family. The story is very funny.
R	**Now listen to Part Two again.**

Answer Key ➤ SB page 79

Test 5

Listening Part 3

In this part, students listen to the dialogue and tick the correct picture.

■ Warm-up

For suggested warm-up activities see Test 1 page 12.

■ Do the test

Materials: SB pages 80 & 81, Audio T5P3

1 Ask students to turn to SB pages 80 & 81. Read the questions and check students know what they mean.

2 Ask students to look at the pictures and check they know the names of the items (objects, places and colours) in them. Take this opportunity to pre-teach any words they may need to know, e.g. *bathroom, tennis, chicken*, etc.

3 Ask students to guess what each dialogue will be about.

4 Play the first part of the recording. Go through the example.

5 Play the rest of the recording and students listen and tick the correct picture.

6 Let students listen to the recording again. Check answers. Ask students to describe one or two of the pictures.

Audioscript

R **Look at the pictures. Now listen and look. There is one example. What's Tony doing?**

M Is Tony watching television in his room?

Mch No he isn't. He's in the kitchen.

M Oh! Is he having lunch?

Mch No. He's making a cake.

R **Can you see the tick? Now you listen and tick the box. One. Where's Jill?**

Part 3
– 5 questions –

Listen and tick (✓) the box. There is one example.

What's Tony doing?

 A ☐

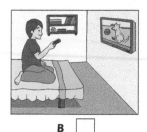 B ☐

 C ✓

1   Where's Jill?

 A ☐

 B ✓

 C ☐

2   What is dad's favourite game?

 A ✓

 B ☐

 C ☐

Fch Mum, where's Jill? She isn't in the kitchen.

F She's in the bathroom.

Fch No she isn't. Oh, I can see her now! She's in the garden.

F Oh, yes. She's playing with the cat.

R **Two. What is dad's favourite game?**

Mch What's your favourite game, dad?

M Well, I don't like football or basketball.

Mch What do you like then?

M Hmm. Tennis.

R **Three. Where's grandpa?**

Fch Dad, dad! Where's grandpa? Is he with you?

M No. He's in the living room.

Fch Is he sleeping?

M No. He's talking to mum.

R **Four. What can Anna have for lunch today?**

Fch Mum, what's for lunch today? Can I have sausages and chips?

F No, sorry Anna. You can have a burger and chips.

Fch Oh, can I have chicken and chips?

F No, I haven't got chicken.

Where's grandpa?

A ☐ B ☐ C ☑

What can Anna have for lunch today?

A ☐ B ☑ C ☐

What's Sam doing?

A ☐ B ☑ C ☐

Test 5, Listening Part 3　81

R **Five. What's Sam doing?**

Mch Who's playing the piano? Is it Sam?

M No. Sam is next to the piano.

Mch Oh, yes. He's talking to a girl.

M No, he isn't. He's singing!

R **Now listen to Part Three again.**

Answer Key ➤ SB pages 80 & 81

Test 5

Listening Part 4

In this part, the students listen and colour items in a picture.

■ Warm-up

For suggested warm-up activities see Test 1 page 14.

■ Do the test

Materials: SB page 82, Audio T5P4, coloured pencils

1 Ask students to turn to SB page 82. Read the instructions.

2 Check students have all the colours they will need.

3 Check students know the name of the items in the picture. Ask them to predict what colour they think each item will be.

4 Play the first part of the recording. Go through the example.

5 Play the rest of the recording and students listen and colour the picture.

6 Let students listen to the recording again. Check answers.

Audioscript

R	**Look at the picture. Listen and look. There is one example.**
F	Look at this picture! Can you see the frogs?
Mch	Yes! There's one between the trees!
F	Well. Colour that frog yellow!
Mch	OK. The frog between the trees is yellow.
R	**Can you see the yellow frog between the trees? This is an example. Now you listen and colour.** **One**
F	There's a frog next to the girl with a hat.
Mch	Where?
F	Next to the girl with a hat. Colour it red.
Mch	Right. That frog is red now.
R	**Two**
Mch	Look at the frog in the bag! It's eating the food!
F	Yes! Green is a good colour for that frog.

Part 4

– 5 questions –

Listen and colour. There is one example.

Mch	Pardon?
F	Colour the frog in the bag green.
Mch	Ok. It's green now.
R	**Three**
F	Now find the frog in front of the flowers.
Mch	Sorry? Where?
F	In front of the flowers.
Mch	Oh, yes. There it is. What colour is it?
F	Colour that frog pink.
Mch	That's funny! A pink frog!
R	**Four**
F	There's a frog on the lion. Can you see it?
Mch	Mmm. Oh yes. I can see it.
F	Ok. Colour the frog on the lion blue.

Mch	Right. I'm colouring the frog on the lion blue.
R	**Five**
Mch	Oh, no! Look! The crocodile is eating a frog!
F	Yes! There's a frog in the crocodile's mouth. Colour it purple.
Mch	What colour?
F	Colour the frog in the crocodile's mouth purple.
Mch	Ok.
F	Well done! It's a nice picture now.
R	**That is the end of Part Five and Test Five.**

Answer Key ➤ SB page 82

Part 1
– 5 questions –

ok and read. Put a tick (✓) or a cross (X) in the box.

ere are two examples.

amples

This is a sock.

This is a leg.

uestions

This is a shell.

Test 5, Reading & Writing Part 1   83

Reading & Writing

Reading & Writing
Part 1

In this part, students look at the picture, read the sentence and put a tick or a cross depending on whether it is true or false.

■ Warm-up

For suggested warm-up activities see Test 1 page 16.

■ Do the test

Materials: SB pages 83 & 84

1 Ask students to turn to SB pages 83 & 84. Read the instructions together.

2 Write the example sentences on the board. Underline the key word in each, e.g. *sock, leg.* Ask students to correct the second example sentence, e.g. *This is a hand.*

3 Students underline the key word in the rest of the sentences and decide if the sentences are correct or not.

4 Ask students to compare answers in pairs.

5 Check answers. Students correct the false sentences. (2 *This is a tiger.* 4 *This is bread.*)

Answer Key ➤ SB pages 83 & 84

Test 5

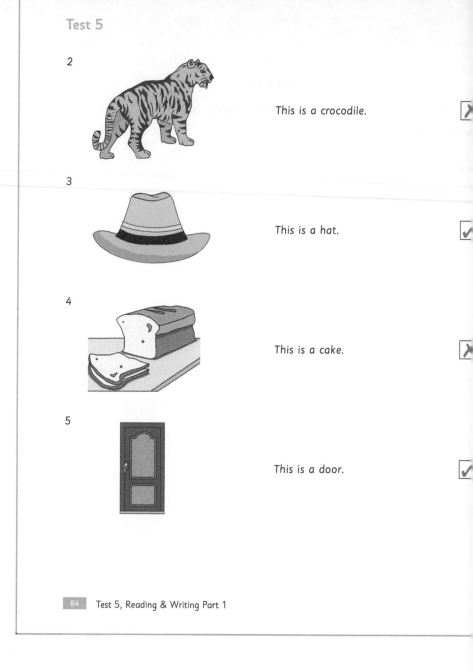

2   This is a crocodile.   ✗

3   This is a hat.   ✓

4   This is a cake.   ✗

5   This is a door.   ✓

Part 2
– 5 questions –

ook and read. Write **yes** or **no**.

xamples

There are two boys in the room.	*yes*
There is a green kite under the bed.	*no*

uestions

One of the boys is reading a book.	*yes*
There is a clock on the wall.	*yes*
There are three apples on the table.	*no*
The doll is between the ball and the cat.	*no*
There is a television on the cupboard.	*yes*

Test 5, Reading & Writing Part 2　　85

Reading & Writing
Part 2

In this part, students look at a picture, read the sentences and then write *yes* or *no*, depending on whether they are true or false.

■ Warm-up

For suggested warm-up activities see Test 1 page 18.

■ Do the test

Materials: SB page 85

1. Ask students to turn to SB page 85. Ask them some questions about the picture, e.g. *How many boys can you see? What colour is the chair?* etc.

2. Discuss the examples together. Ask students to find evidence in the picture to justify the answers.

3. Give students some time to read the descriptions and to check that they match what is happening in the picture.

4. Ask students to compare answers in pairs.

5. Check answers. Students correct the false sentences. (*3 There are two apples on the table. 4 The ball is between the doll and the cat.*)

Answer Key ➤ SB page 85

Test 5

Reading & Writing Part 3

In this part, students reorder letters and write words.

■ Warm-up

For suggested warm-up activities see Test 1 page 19.

■ Do the test

Materials: SB page 86

1 Ask students to turn to SB page 86. Read the instructions carefully. Explain that each dash represents a letter and that the pictures should help them.

2 Write the example on the board. Write both the jumbled letters and the word spelt correctly.

3 Give students some time to unscramble the rest of the jumbled words. Encourage them to cross out the letters after they have used them. Remind them to write only one letter in each space.

4 Ask students to compare answers in pairs.

5 Check answers. Check students have spelt the words correctly.

Answer Key ➤ SB page 86

Part 3
– 5 questions –

Look at the pictures. Look at the letters. Write the words.

Example

door   o r o d

Questions

1

desk   e k s d

2

window    i n w o d w

3

bedroom    d o b r m e o

4

armchair    m a r c i r h a

5

bathroom    t h o m b o a r

Part 4
– 5 questions –

...ad this. Choose a word from the box. Write the correct word next to the ...mbers 1–5. There is one example.

A table

...m in the _____kitchen_____ , the living room and in the
... _____garden_____ too. I am big or small and people sit on
... _____chairs_____ near me. I've got four legs.

...person can put food on me and children can read a **(3)** _____book_____
... me. Dad works on me with his **(4)** _____computer_____ .

...n the **(5)** _____cat_____ sleeps under me.

...hat am I? I am a table.

example

kitchen   tree   cat   book

garden   carrot   chairs   computer

Reading & Writing
Part 4

In this part, students read a text and complete it with the missing words.

■ Warm-up

For suggested warm-up activities see Test 1 page 20.

■ Do the test

Materials: SB page 87

1 Ask students to turn to SB page 87. Read the instructions together. Ask them to say what the text is about. The picture and title will help them.

2 Discuss the example together. Ask them to cross out the word and picture in the box that was used in the example.

3 Give students some time to read the text carefully and to try to choose the best word from the box for each gap. Tell them to read the whole sentence before deciding on the best word for a gap.

4 Ask students to compare answers in pairs.

5 Check answers.

Answer Key ➤ SB page 87

Test 5

Reading & Writing Part 5

In this part, students look at a picture and then write one-word answers to questions.

■ Warm-up

For suggested warm-up activities see Test 1 page 22.

■ Do the test

Materials: SB pages 88 & 89

1 Ask students to turn to SB pages 88 & 89. Ask them to name the items in the pictures. Pre-teach any they don't know.

2 Read the instructions carefully and discuss the examples together. Ask students to point to the parts of the picture that contain the answers.

3 Give students time to read the questions and write the answers. Remind them to write only one-word answers.

4 Check answers after each section. Ask students to compare answers in pairs first. When checking the answers, make sure students have spelt the words correctly.

Answer Key ➤ SB pages 88 & 89

Part 5
– 5 questions –

Look at the pictures and read the questions. Write one-word answers.

Examples

How many children are there? _____ five

Where are the people? at the _____ zoo

Questions

1 Where is the monkey? on a _____ wall

2   What are the girls looking at?   the ___hippos___

3   Who's got the teacher's bag?   the ___monkey___

4   Where is the teacher now?   under the ___tree___

5   What is the crocodile eating?   a ___fish___

Test 5, Reading & Writing Part 5   89

Test 5

Speaking Part 1

In this part, students point to items on the scene picture.

■ Warm-up

For suggested warm-up activities see Test 1 page 24.

■ Do the test

Materials: SB page 93

1 Ask students to turn to SB page 93.
2 Check students know the names of items in the scene picture.
3 Ask them some questions about the scene picture. The students should point to the items rather than describe where each item is, e.g.

Where is the cat?

Where are the pineapples?

Where is the watermelon?

etc.

Speaking Part 2

In this part, students put the object cards in various locations on the scene picture.

■ Warm-up

For suggested warm-up activities see Test 1 page 25.

■ Do the test

Materials: SB pages 91 & 93

1 Ask students to prepare the object cards on page 91 and then turn to page 93 in their SB.
2 Ask students to lay out the object cards on their desk.
3 Give students instructions where to put some of the object cards, e.g.

Which is the mirror?

Put the mirror on the tomatoes.

Which is the hippo?

Put the hippo next to the cat.

Which is the camera?

Put the camera in front of the man.

Which is the mouse?

Put the mouse between the baby and the woman.

etc.

Test 5, Speaking Parts 1–3   93

■ Do the test

Materials: SB page 91

1 Ask students to lay the object cards face up on the table.

2 Ask them questions about the other object cards (the ones not referred to in Part 2), e.g.

What are these? (glasses)

Do you wear glasses? (yes / no)

What are you wearing today? (a skirt)

Speaking Part 5

In this part, students answer personal questions.

■ Warm-up

For suggested warm-up activities see Test 1 page 27.

■ Do the test

Materials: none

1 Ask each student some questions about themselves. They can give one-word answers but encourage them to give a longer answer if they can, e.g.

Who do you sit next to at school? (Mary)

How old is he / she? (10)

Is your teacher a man or a woman? (a man)

Speaking Part 3

In this part, students answer questions about people or things in the scene picture.

■ Warm-up

For suggested warm-up activities see Test 1 page 26.

■ Do the test

Materials: SB page 93

1 Ask students to turn to SB page 93.

2 Ask students some questions about the scene picture. These questions should be ones that the students will need to answer verbally, e.g.

What's this? (a pear)

What colour is it? (green)

How many pears are there? (four)

Where is the girl? (the students point to the girl)

What is she doing? (eating an apple)

Speaking Part 4

In this part, students answer questions about the object cards.

■ Warm-up

For suggested warm-up activities see Test 1 page 26.

Test 5

Speaking frame (Timing = 5 minutes)

What to do (use child's name throughout the test)	What to say	Answer from candidate (one word sufficient)	Back up question if necessary
Usher brings candidate into examination room	Introduces the child to the examiner: *This is …* Examiner to candidate: *Hello my name's ….*	*Hello*	
1 Examiner opens candidate booklet and shows scene to the candidate.	*Look at this. This is a shop. The woman is here with her children.* *This is a bag. (pointing)* *Where is the cat?* *Where are the pineapples?*	Points to items	*Is this the cat? (point)* *Are these the pineapples?*
2 Point to the object cards laid out on the table.	*Look at these, (name).* *Which is the mirror?* *I'm putting the mirror under the clock.* *Now you put the mirror on the tomatoes.* *Which is the hippo?* *Now put the hippo next to the cat.* *Which is the camera?* *Put the camera in front of the man.*	Candidate points. Examiner puts mirror under the clock. Candidate puts card on the tomatoes. Candidate points and puts card next to the cat. Candidate points and places the card in front of the man.	*Where is the clock?* *On the tomatoes.* *Is this the hippo? (points)* *Next to the cat.* *Is this the camera? (points)* *In front of the man.*
3 Remove the cards and point to the scene. Point to a pear. Point the girl. Remove scene picture.	*What's this?* *What colour is it?* *How many pears are there?* *What is the girl doing?*	*Pear* *Green* *Four* *Eating (an apple)*	*Is it a pear?* *Is it brown? Green?* *Are there four? Five?* *Is she eating an apple?*
4 Take 3 object cards not used previously. Close candidate booklet. Show glasses card. Show watch card. Show rice card. Put away all cards.	*What are these? (name)* *Do you wear glasses?* *What are you wearing today?* *What's this?* *Have you got a watch?* *What colour is this / your watch?* *What's this?* *Do you eat rice?* *What do you have for breakfast?*	*Glasses* *Yes / no* *T-shirt and trousers / skirt* *Watch* *Yes / no* *Blue* *Rice* *Yes / no* *Biscuits and milk*	*Are they glasses?* *Are you wearing a t-shirt?* *Is it a watch?* *Is it blue?* *Is it rice?* *Do you have biscuits and milk?*
5 Ask a few personal questions.	*Now, (name). Who do you sit next to at school?* *How old is he / she?* *Is your teacher a man or a woman?*	*My friend / Mary* *10* *Man*	*Do you sit next to your friend?* *Is he / she ten?* *Is your teacher a man?*
	Thank you, (name). *Bye Bye.*		

Worksheet 1

1 Look and match.

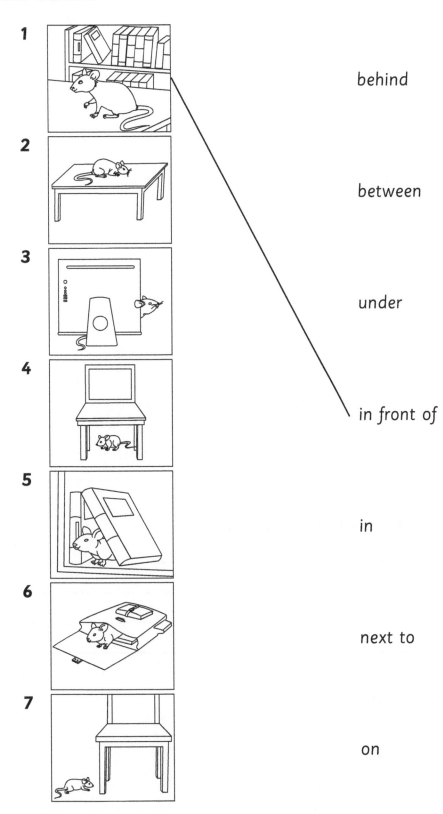

1

2

3

4

5

6

7

behind

between

under

in front of

in

next to

on

Worksheet 2

1 Listen to the names. Tick (✓) the correct column.

	Girl's name	Boy's name	Both girl's & boy's name
Alex			
Ann			
Anna			
Ben			
Bill			
Jill			
Kim			
Lucy			
May			
Nick			
Pat			
Sam			
Sue			
Tom			
Tony			
Dan			
Grace			

2 Listen and write the names you hear.

_____

_____

_____

_____

3 Practise saying the names.

Worksheet 3

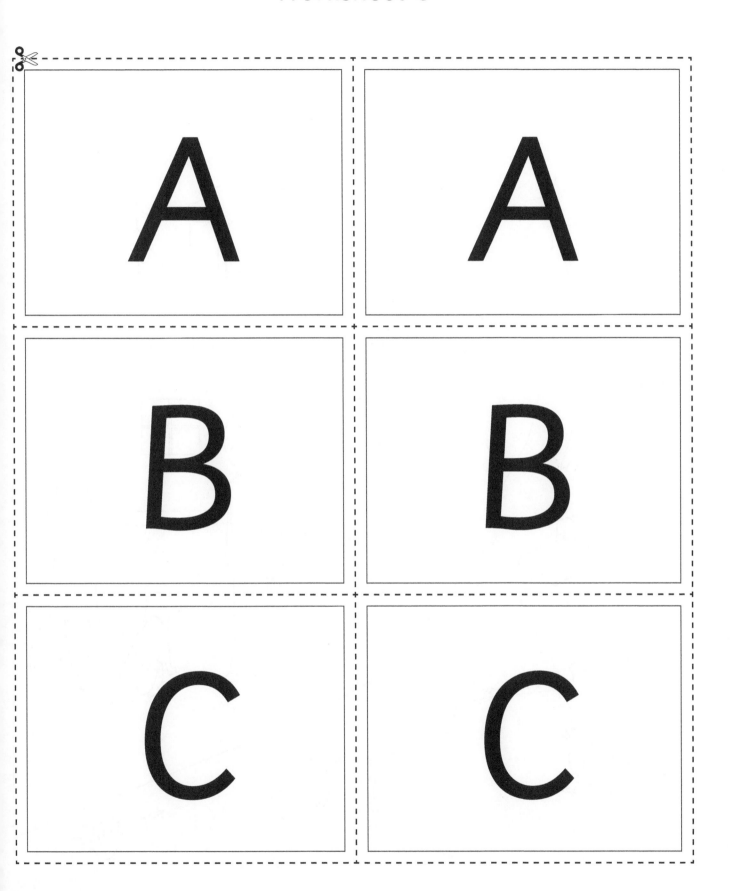

Worksheet 4

Worksheet 5

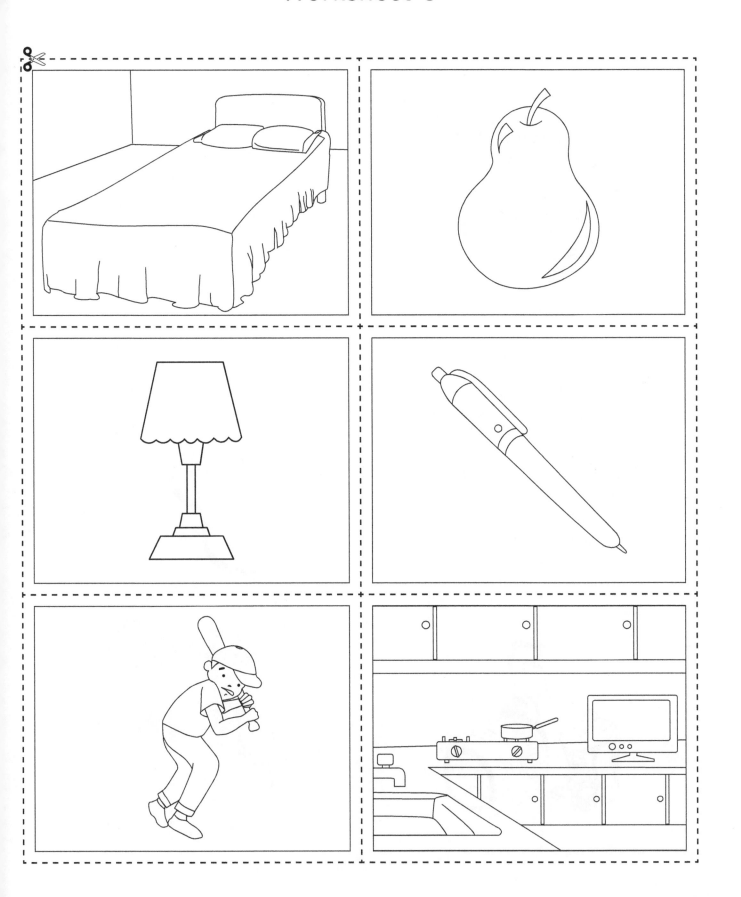

97

Worksheet 6

Worksheet 7

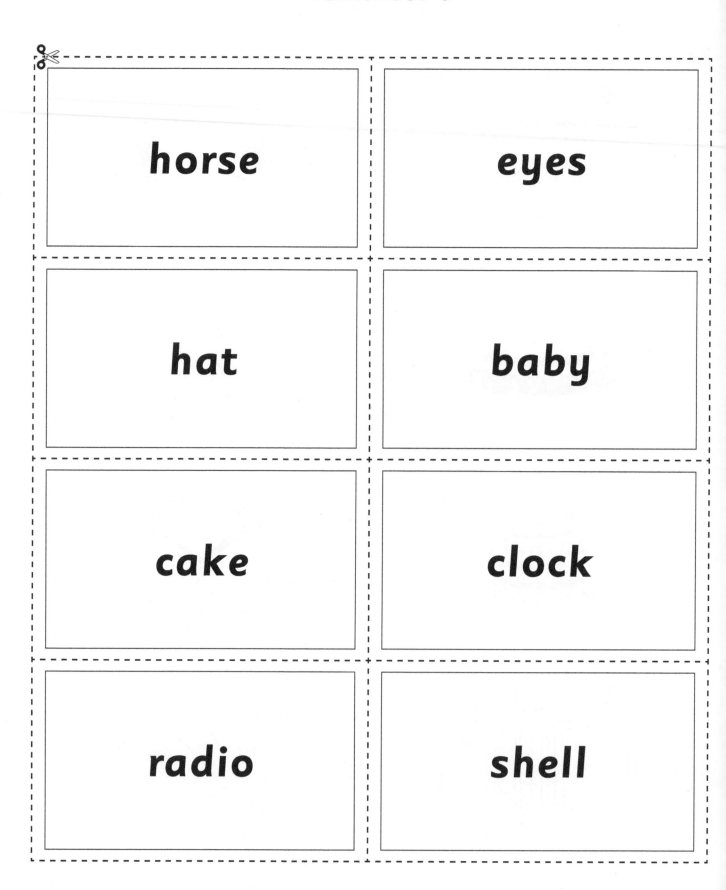

horse

eyes

hat

baby

cake

clock

radio

shell

Worksheet 9

Worksheet 10

Worksheet 11

Read and write the missing words.

A monkey

I live in the _____trees_____ with my family and friends. I play with them a lot.

In the morning I eat a **(1)** _____ . I love it! It's my favourite food.

I am small and I have a long **(2)** _____ . I can run and I can jump,

but I can't use a **(3)** _____ .

I can't read a **(4)** _____ and I don't go to **(5)** _____ .

What am I? I am a monkey.

✂ -

A computer

I am in a school or in a **(1)** _____ . I am on a table or a

(2) _____ . Children sit in front of me. All the **(3)** _____

of the alphabet are on me. **(4)** _____ can learn from me or they can

play **(5)** _____ on me.

What am I? I am a computer.

letters	desk	games	house	children

Worksheet 12

Worksheet 13

1 Look and write the word.

2 Write your own answers.

3 Ask a friend.

a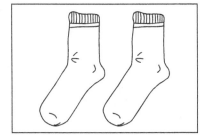

What are these?

They're _____ .

Are you wearing _____ ?

_____

What colour are your _____ ?

_____

b

What's this?

It's a _____ .

Have you got a _____ ?

_____

What's your favourite animal?

_____

c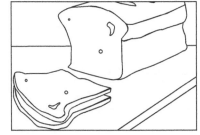

What's this?

It's _____ .

Do you like _____ ?

_____

What do you have for breakfast?

_____

d

What's this?

It's a _____ .

Have you got a _____ in your house?

_____

Where's your _____ ?

_____

Worksheet 14

What's your name?	What's your favourite food?
How old are you?	Is your bedroom big or small?
Have you got any brothers or sisters?	What do you like doing in your bedroom?
How many brothers or sisters have you got?	Can you play table tennis?
How many people are in your family?	Do you like playing sport?
What's your favourite toy?	What sport do you play?
What's your favourite colour?	Do you like watching TV?
Do you like fruit?	When do you watch TV?
What's your favourite fruit?	Have you got a bike?
Do you like chips?	What's your best friend's name?

Starters grammar and structures list

Nouns
Singular and plural including irregular plural forms, countable and uncountable and names
> Would you like an **orange**?
> **Lemons** are yellow.
> Pat has six **mice**.
> I eat **rice** for lunch.
> **Anna** is my friend.

Adjectives
Including possessive adjectives
> He's a **small** boy.
> **His** name is Bill.

Determiners
> It's **a** banana.
> This is **an** apple.
> Put **the** hat on **the** boy's head.
> I want **some** milk.
> **These** books are blue.

Pronouns
Including demonstrative, personal and possessive interrogative pronouns
> **This** is my car.
> Can you see **me**?
> **Which** is Anna?
> Yes, please. I'd like **one**.
> This is **mine**!
> Is that **yours**?

Verbs
(Positive, negative, question, imperative and short answer forms including contractions)

Present simple
> Nick **is** happy.
> I **don't like** eggs.
> **Eat** your lunch!
> **Is** that your sister? Yes, it **is**.

Present continuous (not with future reference)
> What **are** you **doing**?
> The cat**'s sleeping**.

Can for ability
> The baby **can** wave.

Can for requests / permission
> **Can** I **have** some birthday cake?

Have (got) – for possession
> **Have** you **got** a pen?
> She **hasn't got** a dog.

Adverbs
> I'm colouring it **now**.
> My grandma lives here.
> She lives here **too**.

Conjunctions
> I've got a pen **and** a pencil.

Prepositions of place
> Put the clock **next to** the picture.

Question words
> **Who** is that man?
> **Where** is Alex?

Impersonal you
> How do **you** spell that?

Have + obj + inf
> Lucy **has a book to read**.

ing forms as nouns
> **Swimming** is good.
> I like **swimming**.

Let's
> **Let's** go to the zoo.

There is / there are
> **There is** a monkey in the tree.
> **There are** some books on the table.

Would like + v or n
> **Would** you **like to colour** the ball?
> **Would** you like some grapes?

Happy Birthday
> You're eight today! **Happy Birthday!**

Here you are
> Would you like an apple?
> Yes, please.
> **Here you are.**

Me too
> I like football. **Me too.**

So do I
> I love hippos. **So do I.**

story about + ing
> This is a **story about playing football**.

What (a/an) + adj + n
> **What a** good dog!
> **What** beautiful fish!

What now?
> Put the egg in the box.
> OK! The egg is in the box. **What now?**

Starters alphabetic vocabulary list

Grammatical Key

adj adjective

adv adverb

conj conjunction

det determiner

dis discourse marker

excl exclamation

int interrogative

n noun

poss possessive

prep preposition

pron pronoun

v verb

A

a *det*

about *prep*

add *v*

afternoon *n*

again *adv*

Alex *n*

alien *n*

alphabet *n*

an *det*

and *conj*

angry *adj*

animal *n*

Ann *n*

Anna *n*

answer *n + v*

apartment *n* (UK flat)

apple *n*

arm *n*

armchair *n*

ask *v*

at *prep of place*

B

baby *n*

badminton *n*

bag *n*

ball *n*

balloon *n*

banana *n*

baseball *n*

basketball *n*

bath *n*

bathroom *n*

be *v*

beach *n*

bean *n*

beautiful *adj*

bed *n*

bedroom *n*

behind *prep*

Ben *n*

between *prep*

big *adj*

bike *n*

Bill *n*

bird *n*

birthday *n*

black *adj*

blue *adj*

board *n*

boat *n*

body *n*

book *n*

bookcase *n*

bookshop *n*

bounce *v*

box *n*

boy *n*

bread *n*

breakfast *n*

brother *n*

brown *adj*

burger *n*

bus *n*

but *conj*

bye (-bye) *excl*

C

cake *n*

camera *n*

can *v*

candy *n* (UK sweet(s))

car *n*

carrot *n*

cat *n*

catch *v* (e.g. a ball)

chair *n*

chicken *n*

child/children *n*

chips *n* (US fries)

chocolate *n*

choose *v*

class *n*

classroom *n*

clean *adj + v*

clock *n*

close *v*

closed *adj*

clothes *n*

coconut *n*

colour *n + v*

come *v*

complete *v*

computer *n*

correct *adj*

cousin *n*

cow *n*

crocodile *n*

cross *n + v*

cupboard *n*

D

dad(dy) *n*

Dan *n*

day *n*

desk *n*

dining room *n*

dinner *n*

dirty *adj*

do *v*

dog *n*

doll *n*

don't worry *excl*

door *n*

double *adj*

draw *v*

drawing *n*

dress *n*

drink *n + v*

drive *v*

duck *n*

E

ear *n*

eat *v*

egg *n*

elephant *n*

end *n*

English *adj + n*

enjoy *v*

eraser *n* (UK rubber)

evening *n*

example *n*

eye *n*

F

face *n*

family *n*

father *n*

favourite *adj*

find *v*

fish (s + pl) *n*

fishing *n*

flat *n* (US apartment)

floor *n*

flower *n*

fly *v*

food *n*

foot/feet *n*

football *n* (US soccer)

for prep S

friend *n*

fries *n* (UK chips)

frog *n*

from *prep*

fruit *n*

funny *adj*

G

game *n*

garden *n*

get *v*

giraffe *n*

girl *n*

give *v*

glasses *n*

go *v*

goat *n*

good *adj*

goodbye *excl*

Grace *n*

grandfather *n*

grandma *n*

grandmother *n*

grandpa *n*

grape *n*

gray *adj* (UK grey)

great *adj + excl*

green *adj*

grey *adj* (US gray)

guitar *n*

H

hair *n*

hall *n*

hand *n*

handbag *n*

happy *adj*

hat *n*

have *v*

have got *v*

he *pron*

head *n*

helicopter *n*

hello *excl*

her poss *adj + pron*

here *adv*

hers *pron*

him *pron*

hippo *n*

his poss *adj + pron*

hit *v*

hobby *n*

hockey *n*

Starters alphabetic vocabulary list

hold *v*

home *n + adv*

horse *n*

house *n*

how *int*

how many *int*

how old *int*

I

I *pron*

ice cream *n*

in *prep of place + time*

in front of *prep*

it *pron*

its *poss adj + pron*

J

jacket *n*

jeans *n*

Jill *n*

juice *n*

jump *v*

K

keyboard *n* (computer)

kick *v*

Kim *n*

kitchen *n*

kite *n*

know *v*

L

lamp *n*

learn *v*

leg *n*

lemon *n*

lemonade *n*

lesson *n*

let's *v*

letter *n* (as in alphabet)

like *prep + v*

lime *n*

line *n*

listen *v*

live *v*

living room *n*

lizard *n*

long *adj*

look *v*

look at *v*

lorry *n* (US truck)

a lot *adv + pron*

a lot of *det*

lots *adv + pron*

lots of *det*

love *v*

Lucy *n*

lunch *n*

M

make *v*

man/men *n*

mango *n*

many *det*

mat *n*

May *n* (girl's name)

me *pron*

me too *dis*

meat *n*

milk *n*

mine *pron*

mirror *n*

Miss *title*

monkey *n*

monster *n*

morning *n*

mother *n*

motorbike *n*

mouse/mice *n*

mouse *n* (computer)

mouth *n*

Mr *title*

Mrs *title*

mum(my) *n*

music *n*

my *poss adj*

N

name *n*

new *adj*

next to *prep*

nice *adj*

Nick *n*

night *n*

no *adv + det*

nose *n*

not *adv*

now *adv*

number *n*

O

of *prep*

oh *dis*

oh dear *excl*

OK *adj + dis*

old *adj*

on *prep of place*

one *det + pron*

onion *n*

open *adj + v*

or *conj*

orange *adj + n*

our poss *adj*

ours *pron*

P

page *n*

paint *n + v*

painting *n*

pardon *int*

park *n*

part *n*

Pat *n*

pea *n*

pear *n*

pen *n*

pencil *n*

person/people *n*

phone *n + v*

photo *n*

piano *n*

pick up *v*

picture *n*

pineapple *n*

pink *adj*

plane *n*

play *v*

playground *n*

please *dis*

point *v*

potato *n*

purple *adj*

put *v*

Q

question *n*

R

radio *n*

read *v*

really *adv*

red *adj*

rice *n*

ride *v*

right *dis*

right *adj* (as in correct)

robot *n*

room *n*

rubber *n* (US eraser)

ruler *n*

run *v*

S

sad *adj*

Sam *n*

sand *n*

sausage *n*

say *v*

school *n*

sea *n*

see *v*

See you! *excl*

sentence *n*

she *pron*

sheep (s + pl) *n*

shell *n*

shirt *n*

shoe *n*

shop *n* (US store)

short *adj*

show *v*

sing *v*

sister *n*

sit *v*

skirt *n*

sleep *v*

small *adj*

smile *n + v*

snake *n*

so *dis*

soccer *n* (UK football)

sock *n*

sofa *n*

some *det*

song *n*

sorry *adj + int*

spell *v*

spider *n*

sport *n*

stand *v*

start *v*

stop *v*

store *n* (UK shop)

story *n*

street *n*

Sue *n*

sun *n*

supper *n*

sweet(s) *n* (US candy)

swim *v*

T

table *n*

table tennis *n*

tail *n*

take a photo/picture *v*

Starters alphabetic vocabulary list

talk *v*

teacher *n*

television/TV *n*

tell *v*

tennis *n*

test *n + v*

thank you *dis*

thanks *dis*

that *det + pron*

the *det*

their *poss adj*

theirs *pron*

them *pron*

then *dis*

there *adv*

these *det + pron*

they *pron*

this *det + pron*

those *det + pron*

throw *v*

tick *n + v*

tiger *n*

to *prep*

today *adv + n*

Tom *n*

tomato *n*

Tony *n*

too *adv*

toy *n*

train *n*

tree *n*

trousers *n*

truck *n* (UK lorry)

try *n + v*

T-shirt *n*

TV/television *n*

U

ugly *adj*

under *prep*

understand *v*

us *pron*

V

very *adv*

W

walk *v*

wall *n*

want *v*

watch *n + v*

water *n*

watermelon *n*

wave *v*

we *pron*

wear *v*

well *dis*

well done *dis*

what *int*

where *int*

which *int*

white *adj*

who *int*

whose *int*

window *n*

with *prep*

woman/women *n*

word *n*

would like *v*

wow! *excl*

write *v*

Y

year *n*

yellow *adj*

yes *adv*

you *pron*

young *adj*

your *poss adj*

yours *pron*

Z

zoo *n*